MODERN WARFARE

THE IRAQ WAR

An Irish Guards sniper covering a Warrior near the university factory complex in Basra.

MODERN WARFARE
THE IRAQ WAR

Operation Iraqi Freedom
2003-2011

Anthony Tucker-Jones

Pen & Sword
MILITARY

First published in Great Britain in 2014 by
PEN & SWORD MILITARY
an imprint of
Pen & Sword Books Ltd,
47 Church Street,
Barnsley,
South Yorkshire
S70 2AS

ISBN 978 178159 165 9

Typeset by CHIC GRAPHICS

Printed and bound in India by Replika Press

Pen & Sword Books Ltd incorporates the imprints of Pen & Sword
Archaeology, Atlas, Aviation, Battleground, Discovery, Family
History, History, Maritime, Military, Naval, Politics, Railways, Select, Social
History, Transport, True Crime, and Claymore Press, Frontline Books,
Leo Cooper, Praetorian Press, Remember When, Seaforth Publishing
and Wharncliffe.

For a complete list of Pen & Sword titles please contact
Pen & Sword Books Limited
47 Church Street, Barnsley, South Yorkshire S70 2AS, England
E-mail: enquiries@pen-and-sword.co.uk
Website: www.pen-and-sword.co.uk

Contents

Preface

Modern Warfare Series

Pen & Sword's Modern Warfare series is designed to provide a visual account of the defining conflicts of the late twentieth and early twenty-first centuries. These include operations Desert Storm, Iraqi Freedom and Enduring Freedom. A key characteristic of all three, fought by coalitions, is what has been dubbed 'shock and awe', whereby superior technology, air supremacy and overwhelming firepower ensured complete freedom of manoeuvre on the ground in the face of a numerically stronger enemy. The focus of this series is to explain how military and political goals were achieved so swiftly and decisively.

Another aspect of modern warfare is that it is conducted in the full glare of the international media. This is a trend that started during the Vietnam War, and today every aspect of a conflict is visually recorded and scrutinized. Such visual reporting often shapes public perceptions of conflict to a far greater extent than politicians or indeed generals.

All the photographs in this book, unless otherwise credited, were issued by the US Department of Defense and the UK's Ministry of Defence at the time of the conflict. The author and the publishers are grateful for the work of the various forces' combat photographers.

Introduction

Saddam Betrayed

Iraqi President Saddam Hussein declared, in August 2002: 'If they come, we are ready. We will fight them on the streets, from the rooftops, from house to house. We will never surrender.' However, history has a nasty habit of repeating itself, and in his brief to Saddam Hussein on 14 January 1991, General Wafiq Al-Samarrai, head of Iraq's military intelligence, stated that Iraq would suffer a swift defeat. In late March 1991, when the fighting following Operation Desert Storm had finished, Al-Samarrai went before Saddam again to inform him they had suffered the biggest defeat in military history.

One of the Al-Samarrai's successors, former intelligence chief Farouk Hijazi, captured on 24 April 2003, had a similar tale to tell: Saddam would simply not accept that they could not successfully resist the technological array of weapons facing them when the US-led Coalition conducted Operation Iraqi Freedom. By this stage the loyalty of many of Saddam's generals had reached breaking point.

In 2003, in the run-up to war, Washington had many senior military Iraqi exiles it could draw upon, such as General Fawaz al-Shammari, former Chief of Staff of the Iraqi 3rd Corps. Just before hostilities he stated, 'We have good contact with the Iraqi armed forces, the tribes and even some officers in the Republican Guards. They put good hope on the support of the US.' In late November 2002, it became public knowledge that senior Iraqi security officials had approached Washington with a view to abandoning their leader.

American troops burst triumphantly into Saddam International Airport (SIA) and the Rashid military air base, both just outside Baghdad, in early April 2003. Only at the former was there any real resistance and to the Americans' amazement there was no sign of the once powerful Iraqi Air Force (IrAF). Two no shows in three major wars is a remarkable achievement, yet during Operation Iraqi Freedom, as in Desert Storm in 1991, the IrAF decided discretion was the better part of valour. Little was expected of the IrAF in 2003 – after all, it had only put up token resistance twelve years earlier – but no one expected it to vanish completely.

Along with the elite Republican Guard, elements in the IrAF knew they could not avoid the war altogether and sought a way to safeguard themselves and their remaining airworthy fighters. It appears the Americans agreed that if they did not fight, Al Asad – about 170km north-west of Baghdad, and home of the IrAF's Fighter Command and the second largest base in Iraq – would be spared. Secretly across Iraq, the order went out not to resist.

Evidence indicates that the IrAF were either bought off, like the Republican Guard, or simply threatened into submission. US military planners wanted to secure SIA and take out the main Iraqi fighter bases at Al Asad, Al-Taqqadum and Rashid, so they cut a deal with some elements of the IrAF. It is unclear what level of complicity IrAF Commander Lieutenant General Hamid Raja Shalah al-Tikriti had with Washington, but the fact remains that the Iraqis did not put up a single aircraft to resist the Coalition. Intriguingly, unlike the senior Republican Guard and intelligence officers who are believed to have betrayed Saddam Hussein, General Shalah was listed as number seventeen in the US military's 'Iraqi Top 55' most-wanted deck of playing cards.

Intelligence analysts felt that the superior educated air force personnel had a better appreciation of the situation and were viewed as a threat by the very regime that they were supposed to defend. Saddam Hussein knew he faced betrayal. For example, former IrAF General Ali Hussein Habib was arrested just before the Coalition air attacks commenced on Baghdad. His headless body was located on 15 April in a shallow grave outside Abu Ghraib prison. Habib had been involved with the Iraqi Chemical Weapons Programme and was prepared to be interviewed by UN inspectors without minders. It may have been that Saddam's regime suspected he was already collaborating.

On 16 March 2003, at an Iraqi council of war in Baghdad, 150 senior officers, including IrAF General Kareem Saadoun, dared not remind Saddam Hussein they simply could not win. In 1991 the IrAF's pilot training was poor, as was the serviceability of its fighters. On top of this it was operating some fifteen different types of fixed-wing aircraft. Twelve years on, the IrAF was not blind to the fact that these deficiencies had only become worse. The UN embargo ensured they received no vital spares, no new aircraft or surface-to-air missiles, although some spares for Iraqi MiG-23 and MiG-25 may have been sneaked in via Syria.

Once the fighting started, according to some IrAF officers they received no further orders. Colonel Diar Abed at Rashid Air Base noted, 'We had no orders. We just stayed in the bases and waited. … Why don't they give us orders? The leaders at the base didn't know anything.' General Saadoun, also at Rashid, recalled bitterly, 'They just gave us Kalashnikovs [assault rifles], not even anti-aircraft weapons.' Two weeks before Rashid fell, its communications were cut. Somebody, somewhere, had betrayed them. The Coalition blitzkrieg sliced through Iraqi defences and rolled into Basra and Baghdad with relative ease.

The tale of how the Coalition swiftly defeated the Iraqi Army in a matter of weeks, subsequently allowed the country to become ungovernable and then spent almost a decade trying to put it back together again is well trodden. Washington officially said farewell to its military commitment to Baghdad on 31 December 2011. Operation Iraqi Freedom – launched in 2003 to oust President Saddam Hussein – was finally put to rest.

Ultimately, though, Washington and its allies were never in a position to truly remedy Iraq's ills. Like Yugoslavia, it had taken a brutal dictator to hold all the disparate feuding factions together in a single unitary state. While the various former Yugoslav republics were allowed to achieve independence, partition for Iraq was the last thing its neighbours and the international community wanted. Ethnic and sectarian violence are a way of life for Iraq, as are the longstanding tensions with neighbouring Iran. Despite this, Operation Iraqi Freedom remains a remarkable military victory.

In 2003 America and Britain decided Saddam Hussein must go once and for all. America dubbed this military action Operation Iraq Freedom while Britain operated under the codename Operation Telic.

Chapter One

Babylon Lion

Regardless of what the intelligence agencies thought, on the basis of data collected by the UN alone the case for war against Iraq in 2003 seemed irrefutable. The Iraqis had not inconsiderable stocks of chemical and biological munitions that they themselves could not account for and the CIA for a long time estimated that Baghdad had up to 300 Scud ballistic missiles stashed away. On the basis of this Britain and America opted for the conspiracy theory rather than the bugger's muddle theory – i.e. Saddam was deliberately hiding something that constituted a threat.

The Iranians and Kurds had been on the receiving end of his weapons of mass destruction (WMD) in the past and it is widely believed that the only reason Saddam did not use them in 1991 was because America threatened to go 'nuclear'. After the UN inspectors departed Iraq in 1998, Saddam gave the impression he was up to his old tricks. It was a bluff that was to cost him dearly in early 2003.

The Iraqi regular army was believed to consist of about seventeen divisions (each with about 10,000 men) with a total of about 2,200 tanks, 3,800 armoured personnel carriers and 2,000 artillery pieces. In reality these formations were under-strength in terms of equipment, firepower and tactical ability. Even Iraq's elite Republican Guards were no match for Britain and America's modern mechanized forces.

Iraqi Army deployment January 2003
Kirkuk area 1st Corps: 5th Mechanized Division, 2nd, 8th and 38th Infantry Divisions.
Diyala area 2nd Corps: 3rd Armoured Division, 15th and 34th Infantry Divisions.
An Nasiriyah area 3rd Corps: 6th Armoured Division, the 51st Mechanized Division and 11th Infantry Division.
Amarah area 4th Corps: included the 10th Armoured Division, 14th and 18th Infantry Divisions.
Mosul area 5th Corps: 1st Mechanized Division, and the 4th, 7th, and 16th Infantry Divisions.
Western Desert: Armoured Infantry Division and other units in western Iraq.

To defeat Saddam Hussein it was necessary for the Coalition to capture his seat of power, namely the Iraqi capital, Baghdad. It was anticipated that the toughest nut to crack would be the six divisions of his 50,000-strong Republican Guard and their 400-700 tanks. As well as the Guard, the 10,000 Special Republican Guard (SRG) was also regarded as a highly trained and equipped force. Notably, half the Republican Guard Divisions were deployed in an outer ring around Baghdad as the first line of defence.

Iraqi Elite Forces

Republican Guard	Special Republican Guard
50,000 men 6 divisions (3 armoured, 2 infantry, 1 mechanized) 400-700 tanks	10,000 men 4 brigades 100 tanks

Republican Guard Division deployment January 2003

Unit	Location
Nebuchadnezzar	North of Baghdad
Hammurabi	South-west of Baghdad
Al Nida	South-east of Baghdad
Medina-Karbala	Karbala
Baghdad	Al Kut
Adnan	Tikrit

In 1990 Saddam was estimated to have 5,500 tanks, 8,100 armoured personnel carriers (APCs), 500 self-propelled guns and 3,200 pieces of artillery and multiple rocket launchers. Whilst it is impossible to account for all these, visible deliveries of Iraqi armoured vehicle imports from 1953-90 number at least 3,500 main battle tanks (MBTs) and 5,200 armoured fighting vehicles (AFVs). In the aftermath of Desert Storm in 1991, Saddam Hussein still had some 250,000 men remaining under arms equipped with 1,700 tanks, 6,700 APCs and almost 800 pieces of artillery.

Although the Iraqis were left with well over 8,400 armoured vehicles intact, by 2003, after twelve years of sanctions, not all of these were serviceable. In fact, many lay rotting in various Iraqi service depots. In December 2002, a spokesman of the US Army 5th Corps commenting on Saddam's 1991 junkyard at Al-Udairy in Kuwait said, 'I think the strongest message we could send to Mr Hussein right now is to take pictures of this and drop them on Iraq.'

The bulk of Saddam's remaining armoured forces were equipped with Russian-supplied T-54/55, Chinese T-59/T-69, Russian T-62 and some T-72 as well as Russian BMP-1/2 infantry fighting vehicles (IFVs). Only the T-72, known as the Babylon Lion, constituted any kind of real threat to Coalition armour, of which they may have had a few hundred in running order. Iraq commenced the Iran-Iraq War in 1980 with just fifty Soviet-built T-72 tanks. By the end of the war, eight years later, it had managed to acquire approximately 200-500. Reportedly, the Iraqis fielded three variants of the T-72: the Soviet T-72M1 and the T-72B, built at Nizhniy Tagil in what is now Russia, and the T-72G (T-72G/M), built in former Czechoslovakia and Poland. The T-72M1 was a modernized T-72M, which was the export version of the T-72A accepted into Soviet service in 1979. The newer T-72B variant appeared in 1986.

The T-72G was also an export version of the T-72A, built by Poland and Czechoslovakia under the designation T-72M. If it is the case that the Iraqis had T-72Gs then the Czechs and/or Poles may have supplied some of them. Former Czechoslovakia built the T-72 under licence from 1979-93 for both domestic and export markets. Similarly, Poland also manufactured the T-72 under licence until the early 1990s. However, Czechoslovakia was only reported as supplying Baghdad with armoured infantry fighting vehicles and APCs, not tanks. Poland or East Germany are believed to have supplied Iraq with 100 T-55 MBTs in the early 1980s, and 70-100 Polish T-72M1 are known to have been supplied to Iran in the mid-1990s, but not to Iraq.

In the late 1980s, Iraq claimed to be assembling the T-72M1, known locally as the Assad Babyle or Babylon Lion. Iraqi defence industries were producing the ordnance, breech mechanism, ammunition and some of the electronics; the rest was presumably provided as knock-down kits by Russia. Local assembly of the T-72M1 in Iraq is believed to have come to a rapid halt after the 1990-91 Gulf War, due to a lack of parts.

It was only after Saddam's downfall that it became evident what a used car lot Iraq's armoured forces were. The sheer range of suppliers and vehicle types were a logistical and training nightmare that was probably never fully resolved. It transpires the Iraqis also bought armoured fighting vehicles from such diverse countries as Bulgaria, Italy, Hungary, Poland and former Yugoslavia on top of the nine countries previously identified – Austria, Brazil, China, former Czechoslovakia, Egypt, France, Saudi Arabia, South Africa and Spain.

Among the more unusual vehicles supplied to Baghdad during the 1980s was the Hungarian 4x4 PSZH-IV, which apparently was not very mechanically reliable. In comparison to the other East European former Warsaw Pact members (such as Bulgaria, Czechoslovakia, Poland and Romania), Hungary was hardly noted for its manufacture of either Soviet or indigenously designed armoured vehicles. Romania also supplied Iraq with its 122mm APR 40 rocket launcher, carried on a DAC 665T 6x6 truck chassis in the late 1980s.

According to at least one source, Baghdad also imported some ancient Yugoslavian-tracked M-60P APCs. The Italian 4x4 Fiat OTO Melara Type 6614 APC also allegedly found its way into the Iraqi order of battle. This was a joint development between Fiat and Otobreda and was built under licence by South Korea. Whilst by the mid-1990s some 1,160 had been exported, Iraq was not listed as one of the official customers. It is thought possible that some may have come via Somalia or Tunisia.

Many of the 800 Soviet-designed MT-LB multipurpose tracked vehicles acquired by the Iraqi Army were actually built in Bulgaria. The Bulgarians manufactured the MT-LB under licence for both home use and export. The general layout is the same as the Russian versions. However, it is possible that Bulgaria supplied Baghdad with its indigenously designed MT-LB Mortar Carrier variant, which in Iraqi service was modified to carry an Egyptian 120mm mortar. The weapon fires to the rear through an oblong two-part roof hatch, or can be dismounted for ground use.

During the Iran-Iraq War, Kuwait loaned Iraq a battery of at least eight French Giat Industries 155mm Mk F3 self-propelled guns. After the invasion of Kuwait, Iraq captured up to another seventy of them; it is not known how many were subsequently recaptured. Similarly, in 1982, Saudi Arabia loaned Iraq some of its GCT 155mm self-propelled guns to train with while awaiting an order from France. Apparently, self-propelled guns made up 10 per cent of the Iraqi Army's artillery and were only issued to the Republican Guard Corps.

Additional French vehicles supplied included the Panhard VCR (*Véhicule de Combat à Roues*) 6x6 APC, developed as a private venture for the export market in 1975. The Iraqis received 100 of the VCR/TH (Tourelle HOT) anti-tank variant. This was equipped with the Euromissile UTM 800 HOT turret mounted on a raised plinth, capable of carrying four ready-to-launch HOT missiles, with another ten in the hull. As well as the French Panhard 4x4 M3 APC, Iraq also purchased 100 AMX-10P tracked infantry combat vehicles. The production of this model began in 1972 and ended in 1994. Iraqi variants included some with the ATILA automatic artillery fire control system.

After UN sanctions were imposed post-1991, without spares Iraq found it increasingly impossible to maintain its wide range of armoured vehicles. Whilst the Iraqis were able to get some spares on the black market, cannibalization became the name of the game.

By 2003, after years of military sanctions, it was assessed by Western intelligence that the Iraqi Air Force still had approximately 130 attack aircraft and 180 fighters. Of these, only 90-100 were deemed to be operational (MiG holdings may have included thirty MiG-21PF/MF, thirty MiG-23MLs, five MiG-25PDs and four MiG-29s at the end of 2002), enough to thwart any internal unrest but not to take on the might of the United States Air Force (USAF).

The Iraqi Army Air Corps obtained approximately fifty Mi-24 Hind helicopter gunships, of which at least ten were lost in air-to-air combat during the Iran-Iraq War. Allowing for a conservatively similar number lost to Iranian ground fire, only about half those remaining were likely to be serviceable (with the other 50 per cent cannibalized for spares). None were lost in the First Gulf War. This left the Iraqis a fleet of about ten Hinds, sufficient for operations against the Kurds and possible insurrection, but little else. Iraqi Gazelle and BO-105 helicopters were in a similar state. Likewise, it is doubtful that 100 of its transport helicopters such as the Mi-8s were airworthy.

The IrAF learnt an important lesson during Desert Storm; they could not resist or even withstand Coalition airstrikes, and therefore the key to survival was wide dispersal. Hiding places were limited as Coalition intelligence on Iraqi dispersal sites was first class, and the IrAF was only too aware of the danger from Coalition Special Forces ranging far and wide in their search for Saddam and his weapons of mass destruction. One solution to this was deception. The IrAF had a lot of derelict airframes and many of these were placed visibly in revetments as decoys; the challenge for the Coalition was to detect those still operational. The IrAF lost more than 100 aircraft to Coalition military action in 1991; this time round, the battle damage assessment was much harder because of the numbers of Iraqi aircraft that were already little more than junk.

According to General Saadoun, the order to safeguard their aircraft rather than fight was issued in late February 2003, when they began to disassemble and conceal them. The IrAF, along with the Iraqi Army Air Corps (IrAAC), abandoned its air bases and civilian dispersal sites, which were well known to Coalition intelligence and scattered across the width and breadth of the country. Just as in Desert Storm, the IrAF escaped north of Baghdad. This time round though, the IrAF knew better than to flee to Iran, because in 1991 this expedient failed to safeguard precious airframes after Tehran refused to return more than 100 front-line aircraft.

It is also alleged that the Iraqi Air Defence Command (IrADC), operating at 50 per cent of its capacity, also received instructions not to use its radars. Turf squabbles, deliberate or not, stymied the air defence of Baghdad. Some IrADC units were reminded that this was the responsibility of the Republican Guard and ordered not to activate their weapons. Nonetheless, Lieutenant General Muzahim Sa'b Hassan al-Tikriti, the IrADC commander, was number twelve on the Americans' wanted list.

Iraq's armed forces spent two decades buying weapons from around the world, but the bulk of them dated from the Soviet era, such as this BMP-2 infantry fighting vehicle. Its crew abandoned this one once the fighting started; note how the rear portion of the mudguards has been torn off.

Tanks galore – if there was one thing the Iraqis had a lot of in 2003 it was armoured vehicles. Saddam's air force was largely grounded for the lack of spares and his navy was tiny. This meant his main strength lay with his ground forces – in particular, his massed armour such as these T-72 and T-62 tanks.

The formidable Iraqi Babylon Lion that equipped the Republican Guard constituted the main threat to Coalition ground forces. Nonetheless, it was based on a thirty-year-old design dating from the Cold War.

The bulk of Saddam's tanks consisted of the obsolete T-54/55. This particular one was destroyed by the British on the outskirts of Basra.

British troops passing two more knocked-out Iraq T-54s caught on the road to Basra. Both are badly damaged and burnt.

The Iraqis were also equipped with Chinese Type 59 and Type 69 tanks, both a derivative of the Soviet T-54.

Like the Iraqi Air Force, the Iraqi Army had been starved of spares by UN sanctions. As a result, armoured vehicles such as this BMP-1 lay stranded at its depot.

More Iraqi BMP-1s. These were refurbished after Operation Iraqi Freedom for the 9th Mechanized Division.

Rather jubilant Iraqis on their MT-LB multipurpose tracked vehicle. This was another very dated Soviet design. They were built for the Iraqi Army by Bulgaria.

This abandoned BTR-50 amphibious tracked APC was found in the Basra area.

An Iraqi MTLB with an interesting anti-aircraft mount.

A British Royal Marine rigs an Iraqi field gun for destruction. Iraq had about 800 pieces of artillery at the start of the war.

More Royal Marines examining Iraqi anti-aircraft guns, medium machine guns, mortars and rocket-propelled grenades. The Iraqi Army had no shortage of small arms.

Royal Marines assessing piles of captured Kalashnikov assault rifles – this was the standard weapon of the Iraqi infantryman.

The absence of the once powerful Iraqi Air Force in 2003 meant that Iraqi armour suffered terribly on the open road – as these two T-54s testify.

An Iraqi T-72 demonstrating its firepower – this tank performed quite well in 1991, and in 2003 was deployed to defend Baghdad.

Refurbished T-54 and MT-LB on manoeuvres with post-liberation Iraqi mechanized forces.

Chapter Two

Coalition of the Willing

Southern Iraq poses a unique problem to military planners. North of Basra the road to Baghdad is divided by the vast marshes and waterways created by the converging waters of the Euphrates and Tigris rivers, which flow together from Qurna into the Gulf via the Shatt-al-Arab Waterway. The southern route to Baghdad created by the Euphrates runs through the cities of Nasiriya, Najaf, Hillah and Karbala. The northern route following the Tigris passes through Qurna, Amara and Kut. This means any invader coming from the south would have to divide their forces – this was the dilemma faced by the Coalition in 2003.

Under America's Operations Plan (OPLAN) 1003, US Central Command's (CENTCOM) principal blueprint for regime change in Iraq envisaged the initial seizure of Basra, followed by a drive up the Tigris or Euphrates river valleys to Baghdad. This was on the basis that Iraqi forces were assumed to be deployed to delay the capture of Basra – an important jumping-off point for the Coalition – and to disrupt any advance on Baghdad.

The US Marine Expeditionary Force and three British brigades were to be pitched at the city of Basra, while the mechanized US 3rd Infantry Division thrust for Karbala and the US 1st Marine Division for Nasiriyah and Najaf, with Baghdad as the ultimate goal. Elements of the US 101st Airborne Division were also assigned to secure Najaf and defend the long lines of communication.

Throughout the end of 2002 and early 2003, America's military build-up in the Gulf was relentless, with 200,000 troops and perhaps 1,000 MBT/AFVs in the region (Bahrain, Kuwait, Oman, Qatar, Saudi Arabia, Turkey and UAE). Operations were directed from America's As Sayliyah base in Qatar, covering 262 acres and costing $100 million to build, and US CENTCOM in Florida. America had some 3,000 troops equipped with 175 tanks stationed in Qatar. The US Military Sealift Command was busy during this period ferrying in heavy equipment for units such as the US 3rd Infantry Division and the US 1st Cavalry Division.

Gathered in Kuwait were some 30,000 troops and approximately 522 tanks, including the US 3rd Infantry Division (Mechanized) equipped with tanks, IFVs and SPGs. Heavy earth-moving equipment and other specialized vehicles were provided by such units as the US Army's 94th Engineering Combat Battalion, deployed out of Germany. Similarly, the US Army's 19th Support Unit provided pit stop facilities, including, amongst other things, transport vehicle maintenance. Six American camps were strung out along the highway leading north to Iraq, the scene of so much carnage in 1991. Camp Doha outside Kuwait City became home to ranks of Abrams, Bradleys and Paladins. Camp Commando was the base for the US Marines and their tanks, which were expected to be some of the first over the border. All these forces fell under the authority of the US 5th Corps.

The British Armed Forces moved 15,000 vehicles and 9,100 shipping containers to the Middle East in the spring of 2003. The main ground assault formation, 7th Armoured Brigade, was able to field 166 Challenger 2, 236 Warrior, sixty-six Scimitar and thirty-six AS90. The Defence Transport and Movements Agency, part of the Defence Logistics Organization, was responsible for this strategic lift, of which more than 90 per cent was deployed by ship. All military vehicle shipments went via the UK's only military port at Marchwood, located on the western side of Southampton Water. Run by the 17th Port and Maritime Regiment, part of the Royal Logistics Corps, it is tasked with operating ports and beaches all over the world in support of the Armed Forces.

Over the last few years the Royal Navy (RN) and Royal Fleet Auxiliary (RFA) had greatly enhanced their amphibious assault and sealift capabilities. In fact, probably not since the Second World War had Britain had the ability to move such large amounts of armour. HMS *Ocean*, the RN's landing platform helicopter (LPH) that came into service in 1998, can carry up to forty trucks and artillery for the Royal Marines. Fortuitously, the Ministry of Defence had taken delivery of its Strategic Sealift service twenty months ahead of its target date, following delivery of the first three roll-on roll-off (MVs *Hurst Point, Eddystone* and *Hartland Point*) to the contractor in 2002. The following year, four ro-ros shifted some 11 per cent of the equipment needed for the campaign in Iraq. The ro-ros' capabilities are very impressive. Combined, they can move several thousand armoured and unarmoured vehicles. Individually, each vessel can shift up to 8,000 tonnes on three decks. This equates to some 220 vehicles, including Challenger 2 tanks, tracked combat vehicles such as Warrior, FV432, Challenger Armoured Repair and Recovery Vehicle, Sabre, Spartan and the AS90 self-propelled howitzer, as well as support vehicles.

In total, Britain deployed 20-30,000 men, including the 1st Armoured Division (normally stationed in Germany), equipped with Challenger 2 MBTs, and 3,000 Royal Marines, equipped with 130 vehicles, including the Swedish Hagglunds Bv 206 S tracked APC. In late 2002, the Ministry of Defence chartered fifty ferries, including the four large roll-on roll-off commercial vessels, to move them ostensibly for the purposes of conducting military 'exercises' in the Mediterranean. This deployment also gave them access to the Suez Canal. Germany, recognizing the ever-present Iraqi nuclear, biological and chemical (NBC) threat, provided six Fuch biological and chemical detection armoured vehicles, as well as fifty specialists from the 7th NBC Defence Battalion, for deployment in Kuwait.

On the ground and in the air, US firepower was simply overwhelming. Since Operation Desert Storm in 1991, all significant armoured vehicle developments had centred on rebuilds of existing systems such as the M1 Abrams main battle tank, M2 Bradley Infantry Fighting Vehicle and M109 self-propelled gun, although in the case of the M1A2 and M109, they had new turrets. In fact, in recent years there had been no brand-new major systems in production in America except the Lockheed Martin Vought Systems 227mm multiple launch rocket system (MLRS).

America committed 230 MLRS to Desert Storm but by the time of Operation Iraqi Freedom had four times that number available. The system can fire twelve rockets (each containing 640 bomblets) in less than a minute over 32km. American's M1A1 Abrams, of which almost 2,000 were deployed to the Gulf in 1991, had since been replaced by the A2 (both as an upgrade and as a new build), which provided greatly enhanced survivability capabilities. After Desert Storm the US embarked a high-survivability Bradley Modification Plan and the A1s were upgraded to A2 standard. Development of the A3 was also put into train. Bradleys deployed to the Gulf were fitted with explosive reactive armour (ERA), which gives a greater degree of protection from high explosive anti-tank (HEAT) warheads such as the Russian RPG-7.

Likewise under the M109 Howitzer Improvement Programme, the M109 was upgraded to the new A6 Paladin standard. The first ones were completed in 1992, with 630 to be finished by 1998. This gave the M109 a 30 per cent range increase and a 40 per cent operational availability increase. The A6's M284 155mm gun had many improvements, including a 30,000-metre range.

The standard version of the ubiquitous HMMWV (high mobility multipurpose wheeled vehicle), or Hummer, was unarmoured but by the mid-1990s America had started to produce the M1114 up-armoured HMMWV for the US Army and Air Force. To provide better protection and firepower, the up-armouring gives protection against 7.62mm rounds, 155mm overhead airburst and 1.81kg mines. A turret fitting allows the M1114 to carry a 12.7mm or 7.62mm machine gun and 40mm grenade launcher.

The UK fielded the Challenger 2 main battle tank and the AS90 self-propelled gun. After Desert Storm the British Challenger 1 was superseded by the Vickers Defence Systems (VDS) Challenger 2, the first British tank to be designed and built entirely by a contractor since the Second World War. Britain had placed an order in June 1991 for 127 Challenger 2 and thirteen driver training tanks (DTT) and production commenced two years later. An additional 259 tanks and nine DTTs were ordered in 1994. The turret incorporated second-generation Chobham armour and the 120mm rifled tank gun fired a new depleted uranium round with a new propellant system.

In early 1996, Britain phased out its remaining Chieftain MBTs, although the specialized armoured vehicle-launched bridge (AVLB) and armoured vehicle Royal Engineers (AVRE) were retained. The AVLB saw service in the Gulf, whilst the AVRE field prototypes were not completed until 1991.

Also since Desert Storm, the Royal Marines had introduced the Swedish-designed Hägglunds Bv 206 S tracked APC to meet its (ATV) all-terrain vehicle (protected) operational requirement. The Marines were anticipated to acquire up to 160, both as a general troop carrier and for more specialized roles. The Bv 206 D variant of the all-terrain vehicle had already been in service with the British Army for a number of years.

Fire support had been considerably enhanced in the British Army. By the mid-1990s, the British Army had taken delivery of 179 155mm/39-calibre AS90 self-propelled howitzers, built by Vickers Shipbuilding and Engineering Limited (VSEL). They had undergone a mid-life upgrade, some to include a 155mm/52-calibre extended range ordnance and a modular charge system, giving a range of up to 40km. It also fielded 12–16 MLRS with the 39th Heavy Regiment, Royal Artillery (RA) in 1991. In 2003 it had three times that number equipping the 5th, 32nd and 39th Heavy Regiments, RA. In the British Army the MLRS replaced the American M110A2 203mm self-propelled howitzer.

Iraqi opposition forces were also in a position to assist the Coalition, in particular, the CIA recruited up to 5,000 Iraqi exiles for possible missions inside Iraq in support of US combat troops. However, the six main opposition groups were not even able to provide America with 10,000 potential recruits. The two leading opposition groups – the Iraqi National Congress (INC) and the Iraqi National Accord (INA) – had been discredited by their continuing disunity over the years, including the INC's humiliating failure to capture Mosul and Kirkuk in 1995 and the destruction of its infrastructure in Kurdistan the following year (forcing America to evacuate 6,500 survivors).

In the north of Iraq the Kurdish Democratic Party (KDP) and Patriotic Union of Kurdistan (PUK) always found it difficult to bury their long-standing differences to act in any effective manner against the Iraqi military. Furthermore, America claimed it had no plans to use them to wage a proxy war as it did with the Northern Alliance against the Taliban in Afghanistan. The Kurds claimed to have 100,000 fighters, but they probably only numbered a fraction of this and were poorly armed. However, US Special Forces and fighter-bombers were to be involved to help against the Iraqi Army.

Iran's southern Khuzistan Province was home to some 120,000 poor Shi'ite Iraqi migrants. The opposition Iraqi Army of Badr came under the auspices of the Supreme Council for Islamic Revolution in Iraq (SCIRI), an organization based in Tehran under Ayatollah Mohammad Baqir al Hakim. However, in light of its Iranian links, America undoubtedly considered it undesirable.

During the massive Coalition build-up in the Gulf the potential threat stemmed not only from the Iraqi Air Force and Iraqi Air Defence Command, but also from Iraq's coastal defences. Indeed, the primary threat posed by the remnants of Iraqi's tiny navy came from its once extensive armoury of Chinese Silkworm, Soviet Styx, indigenous Faw and French Exocet missiles as well as naval mines. Dramatically, as a prelude to war, Iraqi anti-shipping Silkworm coastal defence missiles were targeted by Coalition air strikes for the first time since the 1991 Gulf War.

American operational staffs decided to eliminate these missiles as they were perceived as a threat to the massing American carrier battle groups (CBGs), amphibious ready groups (ARGs) and the Marine Expeditionary Force (MEF). During early 2003, Western intelligence focused upon, amongst other things, Iraq's residual naval capabilities, particularly the location and readiness levels of its Silkworm anti-ship missiles (ASMs) and its ability to deploy air-launched Exocet ASMs. The Coalition swiftly doubled the number of combat patrols over the no-fly zones and in the south launched a campaign to destroy the residual threat posed by Saddam's remaining coastal and air defences.

Throughout January 2003, Coalition fighters repeatedly attacked Iraqi military communication centres (the air defence command and control site at Tallil, approximately 274km east of Baghdad, the air defence command and control communication facility 8km south-east of Al Haswah, and air defence cable repeater sites located near An Nasiriyah, approximately 274km-east of Baghdad, and between Al Kut, approximately 160km south-east of Baghdad, and Basra, 450km south-east of Baghdad), and mobile radars (located near Al Qurnah, approximately 209km south-east of Baghdad, and near Al Amarah, 266km south-east of Baghdad). These raids were designed to blind and disable the Iraqi Air Defence Command (IrADC) in the run-up to an invasion. They also dropped millions of leaflets across southern Iraq.

At the end of January an anti-aircraft artillery (AAA) site near Tallil was bombed. Then, in February, the Coalition began targeting Iraq's mobile surface-to-air missiles (SAMs) as well, principally near Basra and An Nasiriyah, belonging to the IrADC, Iraqi Army and Navy. Mobile air defence early warning radars located near Basra, An Nasiriyah and Ar Rutbah (approximately 402km south-west of Baghdad), which provided intelligence to the IrADC, were also hit.

During early 2003 in the Northern Watch area, Coalition aircraft regularly 'lit up' air defence sites and dropped leaflets in the region of the northern city of Mosul. On 31 January, Coalition fighters launched precision-guided munitions (PGMs) in self-defence against Iraqi AAA, approximately 16km east of Mosul. Also, on 25 February, Northern Watch patrols attacked three SAM systems some 10km south of Mosul. Two days later, they struck three different fibre-optic cable and microwave communication sites supporting Iraqi military operations, located approximately 24km west and 29km south of Mosul.

In the first week of March 2003, under the pretext of enforcing the no-fly zones more vigorously, elements of USAF's Air and Space Expeditionary Forces (AEFs – assigned to Northern and Southern Watch) fighter-bombers directed by CENTCOM and the Combined Air Operations Centre at Prince Sultan Air Base (Saudi Arabia) began to again strike Iraqi coastal defence positions in the southern no-fly zone. These particular missile sites had been kept under constant surveillance by the British Naval Task Group since 1999. The Iraqis prudently refrained from activating their fire-control radars regularly and for the time being had been given a stay of execution by patrolling British and American warplanes.

Attacks were conducted by US air wings based in Saudi Arabia, Kuwait, Qatar and with the USS *Constellation* (CVN 64) and *Harry S Truman* (CVN 75) CBGs. Strike aircraft included carrier-based F-14D Tomcats, F/A-18C/E/F Hornets and EA-6B Prowlers, and land-based F-15 and F-16. US airpower had been greatly enhanced by the deployment of elements of the 7th, 8th, 9th and 10th AEFs.

Notably, the 9th and 10th AEFs included F-15C Eagles from Langley Air Force Base's (AFB) 1st Fighter Wing and F-16s from Spangdahlem in Germany. Elements of USAF's 4th Fighter Wing, from Seymour Johnson AFB, deployed to Qatar, also with their F-15E Strike Eagles. The 7th and 8th AEFs included B-1B Lancer bombers, from the 28th Bomb Wing Ellsworth AFB, deployed to Oman. Strategic support for the B-1Bs was provided by the venerable B-52s from Barksdale AFB, Louisiana, which were deployed to Diego Garcia (in the Indian Ocean) and Britain's RAF Fairford. Other American aircraft in the region included F-117A Nighthawks and US Marine Corps F/A-18.

By the spring of 2003 the Coalition were targeting all of Iraq's mobile missile systems after anti-ship missiles, surface-to-surface missiles, surface-to-air missiles, and early warning radars moved provocatively, some might argue foolishly, into the southern no-fly zone. Due to growing concerns these systems could be within range of American forces in Kuwait or Saudi Arabia, air strikes were launched immediately they were located by intelligence and reconnaissance sorties.

The tempo of Coalition sorties rose dramatically to about three times what they had been before; reportedly, up to 750 a day were being flown by all types of aircraft. In the first few days of March, American and British fighters attacked five air defence targets in the southern no-fly zone in 'response' to AAA fire. There were additional reports of Coalition aircraft striking rocket launchers and SAMs (specifically the Ababil-100, which could allegedly lay batches of mines in front of advancing tanks) as well as coastal defence missiles. In further raids near Basra, American warplanes attacked military communications facilities and an air defence battery that fired on them.

Additionally, during the first week of March USAF dropped one and half million leaflets in the Southern Watch area, warning the Iraqis not to resist. On 1 March in the Northern Watch area, they dropped a quarter of a million leaflets alone on just two AAA sites 16km north-east of Mosul. These warned: 'Any hostile action by Iraqi air defences towards Coalition aircraft will be answered by immediate retaliation.'

In order to carry out the invasion of Iraq, sealift capabilities were vital. HMS *Albion* (seen here) and HMS *Bulwark*, were two new assault ships that had recently joined the British fleet, capable of moving up to sixty vehicles, including a mix of six Challenger 2 tanks and thirty Viking all-terrain vehicles.

HMS *Ocean* and HMS *Albion*, the former the RN's Landing Platform Helicopter (LPH), can carry up to forty trucks and artillery for the Royal Marines.

A British Warrior armoured combat vehicle with 7th Armoured Brigade deploying to the Gulf in February 2003, onboard the MV *Longstone* at Emden, Germany. Defeating Saddam Hussein required logistical support on a massive scale.

Fresh from Germany, a British Challenger 2 being delivered in Kuwait ready for Operation Telic in 2003 – clearly it has yet to be painted desert sand for the coming campaign.

Two rusty looking Challenger armoured repair and recovery vehicles just offloaded in Kuwait.

Vehicles unloaded from container ships at the port of Kuwait form up in convoy ready for their journey to logistic and front-line units supporting Operation Telic, the British element of Operation Iraqi Freedom.

A freshly painted British AS90 155mm self-propelled gun of 3 Royal Horse Artillery being loaded at the German port of Emden.

The 7th Armoured Brigade on the move. Note the gaping doors of the ro-ro. Few countries apart from America have such sealift capabilities when it comes to moving armoured formations around the world.

America easily has the largest military sealift fleet in the world. US Army Humvees, or Hummers, are loaded onto the large, medium-speed ro-ro USNS *Pililaau*.

An assortment of US Marine Corps Abrams tanks and amphibious assault vehicles on the USS *Rushmore* (LSD 47) in the Gulf of Oman. The USMC is a self-contained fighting force with its own assault ships, carriers, aircraft, helicopters, tanks and AAVs.

A British Warrior being offloaded from a low-loader in the Middle East.

British Paras in Kuwait on 23 February 2003 deploying in the Land Rover Weapons Mounted Installation Kit, or WMIK. These vehicles carry .50 calibre Browning heavy machine guns, 7.62mm general purpose machine guns and Milan anti-tank missile systems.

British Challenger 2 of the 1st Armoured Division outside Basra. The UK sent about 100 of these tanks to Iraq.

British Warrior ACVs on manoeuvres with the 1st Royal Regiment of Fusiliers Battlegroup in Kuwait in mid-March 2003.

Members of the Irish Guards photographed on 27 March 2003 taking a break in southern Iraq.

The US M1A2 Abrams was an upgraded version of the M1A1, which had first seen combat in Iraq in 1991. In 2003 it deployed to Iraq with both the US Army and USMC.

The US M2 Bradley Infantry Fighting Vehicle provided armoured transport for America's mechanized forces.

The venerable US M113 also saw combat in Iraq. This column was photographed in 2005 as part of the follow-on forces.

The US High Mobility Multipurpose Wheeled Vehicle, or HMMWV or HUMVEE. Known as the Hummer by US troops, this vehicle was deployed to Iraq in both unarmoured and armoured versions.

As well as a vast array of jets, Coalition forces were supported by the battle-proven AH-64 attack helicopter armed with a chain gun, rockets and guided missiles.

Abrams crews ready themselves for action; their key objectives were Basra and Baghdad – they had to take on around a dozen Iraqi armoured and mechanized divisions.

The US 155mm M109 A6 Paladin self-propelled howitzer provided vital fire support, particularly against strongpoints around Iraqi cities.

Challengers on the road to Basra.

The British 7th Armoured Brigade included thirty-six AS90 self-propelled guns serving with the Royal Horse Artillery; these ones are firing on Basra.

British troops in WMIKs on the outskirts of Basra.

The war in Iraq was characterized by the extensive use of unmanned aerial vehicles, or drones. The US Global Hawk surveillance UAV flew in support of Operation Iraqi Freedom.

An M2A2 serving with the US 3rd Infantry Division in Iraq fitted with appliqué passive armour rather than the explosive reactive armour system.

Chapter Three

Marines Storm Basra

Basra – Iraq's second-largest city and main seaport – lies (according to Iraqi figures) 67km from the Gulf, 549km from the Iraqi capital and 50km from the Iraqi-Kuwaiti border. The Tigris and Euphrates rivers join near Baghdad and then part again before meeting to the south at Qurna to form the Shatt-al-Arab River, or Waterway, which flows through Basra and on into the Gulf. The Shatt-al-Arab was reportedly navigable by maritime traffic for about 130km (the channel had been dredged and was reportedly in use), though was littered with junk and unexploded ordnance from the Iran-Iraq and Gulf War conflicts.

Other Iraqi ports were just not up to the job. Al-Faw (Fao), Khawar al Amaya and Mina al Bakr are just oil terminals, whilst Khor al-Zubair (Khawar az Zubayr) is an industrial port. Along with Umm Qasr, they all have one thing in common: their harbours are too small to conduct effective military operations from and geographically they are too far south to assist with a push on Baghdad. Umm Qasr on the Gulf is where goods from the oil-for-food programme underwent UN scrutiny, while the UN-approved oil was exported from Mina al Bakr. In contrast, Basra's facilities had become a haven for smugglers. Khor al-Zubair to the north of Umm Qasr was dredged in the late 1980s to allow access for medium-sized bulk carriers, but was still inadequate.

The capture of Basra, along with its docks, was vital to a successful invasion of Iraq. Any attack was likely to be three-pronged; certainly from the south up towards Barsa and Nasiriya and then Baghdad; possibly from the west across the Syro-Arabian desert from Saudi Arabia towards Najaf and Karbala and on to Baghdad; and possibly from the north from Turkey down the road from Zakho to Mosul and Kirkuk, and across the upper plain towards Baghdad. In the event, Saudi Arabia and Turkey did not want to be party to the assault on Iraq. Of the three, Basra became the jumping-off point for any assault on the Iraqi capital. Also, opposition to Saddam's Sunni-based regime could rally on the Shia Muslims of Basra.

The city consists of three main areas – Ashar, Margil and Basra proper. The latter is the old residential area to the west of Ashar, while Ashar itself consists of the old commercial district, including the Corniche running along the Shatt-al-Arab, Sharia al-Kuwait and Sharia ath-Thawra. The Shatt-al-Arab is dominated by Sinbad Island, connected to Basra by a bridge. To the north-west of Ashar is Margil. This is strategically the most important district as it contains the port and the railway station (the 582km Umm Qasr Line), which links the city with Baghdad. Basra also has an international airport, closed to international traffic since 1990, and a nearby petrochemical complex.

Basra's estimated two million people lived largely in a state of chaos. The city's infrastructure was a shambles and suffered chronic power cuts, with leaking sewage and water networks. Criss-crossed by waterways and canals, the Iraqis once called it the 'Venice of the East'. However, the city and the port were in an extremely poor state of repair. Both suffered extensive damage in the war with Iran, the Gulf War and the subsequent 1991 Shia rebellion.

The port, which needed dredging, was described as a 'crumbling Third World dustbin'. The quays and wharves were in a state of disrepair and were cluttered with derelict vessels, most of them victims of the Iranians rather than the Americans, as the locals claimed. The canals were fetid and many blocked with old tyres and concrete debris. The Shatt-al-Basra Canal was navigable by shallow-draft craft until 1991. The Venetian-style bridges lay in ruins. Similarly, the Shatt-al-Arab itself was littered with vessels that were the victims of the Iran-Iraq War. The railway line was overgrown and the marshalling yard filled with long-abandoned trucks.

To the north of Basra, encompassing the southern governorates of Basra itself, Thi Qar and Misan were once vast marshes covering 10,000km^2. However, much of them was drained in the late 1980s. Also, 74km north of Basra lies Qurna (the Garden of Eden, as legend has it) on the confluence of the Tigris and the Euphrates. Beyond Qurna is Amara, where the Iraqis built new docks in the 1980s. All three cities are linked by a good highway that goes all the way to the capital. To the west of the marshes and Qurna is Nasiriyah, some 375km south-east of Baghdad, which again sits astride a highway going north.

In the run-up to war, Royal Navy mine hunters were charged with mine-clearing operations in the northern Gulf and opening the approaches to the Shatt-al-Arab leading to Basra and the Euphrates river system. In order to take Basra, the Coalition needed to secure Al-Faw, a sizeable city at the mouth of the Shatt-al-Arab that remained a ruin after being captured by the Iranians in 1986. An amphibious force was prepared for such a role and included the Royal Marines and US Marine Corps.

It was anticipated that all the bridges over the Tigris and the Euphrates would be destroyed to delay any forces seeking to cross en route to Iraq's cities until more Iraqi troops could be deployed southward. The Iraqis would also probably attempt to destroy Basra's port facilities rather than let them fall into Coalition hands.

Basra was defended by what the Iraqi Army called 'Saddam forces', or the Popular

Army (little more than militia), and elements of the Republican Guard from several divisions (a tougher nut to crack). On paper the Iraqi garrison looked formidable. General Ali Hassan al-Majid, Saddam's cousin, had up to 2,000 naval personnel, with half a dozen missile-armed patrol boats, 10,000 troops of the army's 51st Mechanized Division, with armour, miscellaneous air defence forces, irregular Fedayeen (men of sacrifice) and units of the Republican Guard. Up to another 30,000 men of the 10th, 12th and 14th Iraqi divisions were deployed in the region.

Security in the city remained tight due to the threat of invasion and because the regime did not trust the Shia population. Basra's air defences were also quite extensive, though continued to suffer in air raids. Any Coalition naval push up the Shatt-al-Arab would almost certainly be accompanied or pre-empted by a swift airborne assault that would seek to seize the airport, docks, highway and Sinbad Island before the Iraqi defenders could react.

General al-Majid's options were fairly limited; he did not want to get his mechanized division entangled in the streets of Basra, which meant holding the city would fall largely to the militia and other ramshackle volunteer formations. He must have known that his dug-in supporting infantry units were unlikely to withstand the Coalition's mechanized units and fighter-bombers once they pressed home their attacks.

At best he must have hoped he could suck Coalition forces into Basra, where they would be forced to fight costly urban warfare that would hold up their advance. His regular forces could conduct local counter-attacks designed to cut off Coalition troops once they were inside the city. The reality was that this would be a tall order in the face of concerted attacks by enemy jets, helicopter gunships, missiles and artillery. Such firepower would make it almost impossible for him to concentrate his tanks for a counter-attack.

It is doubtful that General al-Majid received very much, if any, intelligence regarding the forces facing him. At army and corps level air attack had largely blinded the Iraqi armed forces. No doubt spotters using mobile phones relayed some information to his commanders but this will have provided little information other than to confirm approaching enemy troops. He must have appreciated that once the attack commenced his men would be subject to the full firepower that modern western armies can muster.

The countryside south of Basra had been the scene of heavy fighting in 1991, when Saddam's Republican Guard took a pounding in the 'Basra Pocket'. The Guard had eventually escaped north but not before they had been subjected to a gruelling air attack and involved in bitter tank battles with the Americans. This time the Republican Guard Corps was far to the north, defending Baghdad – General al-Majid was essentially on his own.

It's likely that General al-Majid looked at his situation maps and appreciated that the Coalition would not want to get bogged down in Basra so would bypass it. There was every likelihood that he and his garrison would be trapped by a holding force while American and British tanks fought their way to the capital. His was a thankless and unenviable task.

The first confirmed firefight between American and Iraqi forces took place on 20 March 2003, 3.57 pm local time. LAV-25s (light armoured vehicles), armed with 25mm cannon, from the 3rd Light Armored Reconnaissance Battalion, US 1st Marine Division, engaged two Iraqi armoured personnel carriers south of the border. The LAV-25s swiftly destroyed the Iraqi forces using chain guns and TOW (tube-launched, optically-tracked, wire-guided) anti-tank missiles.

Afterwards, the first units of the powerful US 3rd Infantry Division, equipped with 200 M1A2 Abrams, 260 M2 Bradleys, fifty-four M109 Paladins and twenty-four Apache AH-64 helicopter gunships, crossed into Iraq, engaging and destroying an Iraqi command post and two T-72s.

Under covering fire from the 'Desert Rats' of Britain's 7th Armoured Brigade, units from the 26 Armoured Engineer Squadron spearheading the attack pierced the Iraqis' sand berms and laid bridging equipment to allow US Marine Abrams to pass through the Iraqi border. Prior to this, 155mm artillery and US Marine Cobra helicopter gunships had pounded positions held by the Iraqi 51st Mechanized Division.

Two days later, the US 1st Marine Division drove on to Basra. While securing the oil fields outside of the city they stumbled upon ten Iraqi T-55 tanks dug into defensive positions. Using shoulder-launched missiles and TOWs mounted on top of their 4x4 HMMWVs, the Americans destroyed all of them. A massive British contingent of about 8,000 troops, 120 tanks and 145 armoured vehicles also moved into southern Iraq from Kuwait to support US forces heading for Basra. They soon found themselves coming into contact with regular Iraqi Army forces, including the 51st Division. The 10th, 12th and 14th Iraqi divisions were also reportedly in the region.

Iraqi reinforcements, believed to be a mix of regular troops from the 51st and irregular troops, also moved into Basra from the north. In one reported incident the Royal Scots Dragoon Guards (RSDGs) had to retire 16km to avoid potential ambush by Republican Guards heading out of Basra.

Despite a complete lack of air cover the Iraqis launched two counter-attacks on 24 March 2003 involving up to fifty armoured vehicles, losing twenty elderly T-55 tanks in the process. In the first, British AS90s of the Royal Horse Artillery accounted for eleven Iraqi vehicles, including artillery and tanks. Some T-55s were destroyed in the southern suburb of Abu al Khasib, just 5km from Basra. The second attack was broken up by Harriers, which accounted for twenty Iraqi armoured vehicles heading for al-Zubayr.

On 26 March it was claimed British forces were involved in the biggest tank battle since the Second World War when a convoy of up to 120 Iraqi armoured vehicles tried to break out of Basra. The MoD later clarified there had only been three vehicles! Additionally it was reported that fourteen Challengers of the RSDGs moving east to reinforce the Royal Marines came across a column of fourteen Iraqi T-55 and four APCs. The Guards claimed more than a dozen of them.

On 29 March, the Household Cavalry Regiment found itself in a stand-off with an Iraqi tank and APC until an Army Air Corps Lynx Mk7 destroyed the APC and drove off the tank. The following day in Operation James (after Bond), 600 Royal Marines from 40 Commando attacked Abu al Khasib. The bitter battle, fought against an enemy force of mixed composition and determination, numbering around 500 and bolstered by several squadrons of T55 tanks, lasted for almost thirteen hours.

British AS90s were called in to deal with twenty-one Iraqi vehicles, some believed to be T-55 tanks, to the north of the Shatt-al-Arab, posing a threat to 40 Commando. Coalition drones spotted the build-up and afterwards the AS90 barrage CENTCOM showed images of all the vehicles either destroyed or damaged beyond repair. To the north-west of Basra, on 31 March, a build-up of some 200 Iraqi troops and twenty-five tanks were also destroyed in well co-ordinated airstrikes. This marked the end of General al-Majid's concerted efforts to hold Basra.

Three elements of the 7th Armoured Brigade moved cautiously towards the city from positions to the west. The RSDGs drove in with their Challenger 2, while 1st Battalion, the Royal Regiment of Fusiliers, and 1st Battalion, the Black Watch, went in aboard their Warriors. Later in the day, 3 Commando Brigade began another push forward from positions south of the city.

By 3 April, the RSDGs were pressing on the outskirts of Basra, when six Challengers and fifteen Warriors, supported by Lynxes, drove the Iraqis from a derelict agricultural college, destroying a T-55 in the process. The following day, five Challengers and five Warriors drove Iraqi militia from the shanty town of Cobla, one Challenger sustaining a direct hit by a rocket-propelled grenade (RPG) but suffering no ill effects.

It was anticipated that the Iraqis would destroy Basra's port facilities rather than let them fall into Coalition hands. Similarly, the bridges over the Tigris and the Euphrates would be destroyed to delay forces seeking to reach Iraq's other cities. In the event, British armour and Coalition aircraft successfully dealt with the garrison. Basra's navy was sunk along the Shatt-al-Arab and after several foolish forays the 51st's armour was left strewn along the highway to the south. General al-Majid was reported killed on 6 April in an air strike and the following day Britain announced that Saddam's rule over Basra was at an end, 1,000 hardcore loyalists having been driven out. The city's facilities fell into Coalition hands 'intact'.

To the far north, US armour, spearheading Operation Thunder Run, entered Baghdad on 5 April 2003, heralding the beginning of the end for Saddam's regime. The Iraqi capital was always seen as the centre of gravity, which is why Coalition strategy utilized blitzkrieg-style tactics, slicing through Iraqi defences and pressing on regardless of what was happening on their flanks.

Queen's Dragoon Guards' Scorpion and Spartan in the Kuwaiti desert in mid-February 2003. These vehicles have only been partially over-sprayed with sand to give them a camouflaged pattern.

The lull before the storm: members of 40 Commando on the British flagship HMS *Ark Royal* photographed late on 21 March 2003. Their job was to secure Al Faw and Umm Qasr ready for the push on Basra.

British Challenger 2 tanks were instrumental in the drive on Basra. This tank belongs to the Queen's Royal Lancers and is crossing a bridge from Kuwait into Iraq on 21 March 2003.

A WMIK of the 1st Battalion Royal Irish Regiment passing burning Iraqi oil wells on 22 March 2003.

More men of the
Royal Irish Regiment
moving into Iraq on
22 March.

Troops from 40
Commando take
up positions
during operations
to secure Al Faw
and Umm Qasr.

British Paras
securing an Iraqi
pipeline before
more sabotage
could take place.
This man's small
arm is the SA80 or
L85 5.56mm asault
rifle.

1st Royal Regiment of Fusiliers with a Milan anti-tank weapon on the outskirts of Basra on 25 March.

British AS90s bombarding Basra's defences on 28 March.

Commandos from 42 Commando being flown into the Umm Qasr area on 29 March 2003 by Naval Air Squadrons operating from HMS *Ocean*.

Tough and well-armed Commandos in the Umm Qasr area. These operations caught the Iraqis almost completely off guard.

A Royal Marine stands guard alongside a torn poster of Saddam Hussein outside 3 Commando Brigade's HQ in Umm Qasr.

A Royal Marine Gazelle helicopter patrolling the Umm Qasr area.

A British hovercraft patrols the Shatt al-Arab Waterway. The marine at the window is armed with the squad automatic weapon version of the SA80, known as the L86.

This fusilier is monitoring Iraqi defensive positions outside Basra. Note the mix of jungle and desert disruptive pattern material, or DPM, with his uniform.

Early April 2003, a Para mortar team engages Iraqi targets. The mortar round is just visible, having left the tube.

An Irish Guards sniper covering a Warrior near the university factory complex in Basra. From this Iraqi stronghold British forces had to endure small arms, mortar and even surface-to-air missile fire.

Twenty-one days after the invasion of Iraq, 42 Commando trudge though Basra, supported by British Challenger 2s.

A British Challenger supported by a US Marine Seacobra probes Basra's defences near Saddam's palace.

Kicking-in the door – Royal Marines of 42 Commando burst into Saddam's Basra palace on 7 April 2003. Like many of the government buildings, it was deserted.

A Royal Scots Dragoon Guards Challenger driving through Basra in support of 3 Commando Brigade. By this stage organized Iraqi resistance in the area had all but collapsed.

A young Iraqi cyclist takes his own life in his hands riding by a Queen's Royal Lancers Challenger guarding the Fusiliers' HQ in the Shatt al-Arab Hotel, Basra.

Iraqi children welcome a Queen's Dragoon Guards Scimitar crew in the city of Basra.

British light reconnaissance tanks on the streets of Basra late at night prior to securing Saddam's palace.

On garrison duties, a Saxon armoured patrol vehicle on the streets of Basra, with the 1st Battalion Queen's Lancashire Regiment.

British reinforcements – Warriors of the Princess of Wales Royal Regiment in Iraq poised for action.

British machine gunners practising off the back of a Saxon.

Chapter Four

Sixteen Days to Baghdad

Despite the rapidity of the fall of Baghdad the Coalition victory was by no means a complete pushover. In places the Iraqis fought bravely and stubbornly to keep out the invaders. The US Marines, in trying to secure the three key bridges over the Euphrates at Nasiriyah, met stiff resistance from regular Iraqi Army units and Fedayeen militia. The intention was to approach from the southeast to secure a bridge over the river, then north through the outskirts to the canal bridge and then turn west to secure a second canal crossing. This would open the most direct routes to Baghdad.

Nasiriyah was the headquarters of the Iraqi Army's 3rd Corps, consisting of the 11th Infantry, 51st Mechanized and 6th Armoured divisions, which were only at about 50 per cent strength. The 51st operated south, covering the oilfields, and the 6th was north, near Al Amarah, which left three brigade-sized units – the 23rd, 45th and 47th of the 11th Infantry Division – plus elements of the 21st Tank Regiment to guard the Nasiriyah area and the bridges over the Euphrates. The 45th Brigade was to prove one of the most proficient units and Iraqi defences in the area of the Saddam Canal were particularly tough.

The initial plan was for the Marines' Task Force Tarawa to seize and hold the two bridges inside Nasiriyah, holding open a corridor for Marine Regimental Combat Team 1 to pass north through the city along Route 7. This immediately went awry when a US maintenance unit got lost and bumped into the Iraqis' defences, triggering a lengthy firefight. Task Force Tarawa then had to go to their rescue. Only then could the attack be launched into the south of the city.

In a scene reminiscent of the Second World War, the Marines assaulted the first bridge, using twenty amphibious assault vehicles (AAVs), several Abrams tanks and ten HMMVWs equipped with TOW missiles. The way was cleared by Marine Corps Cobra helicopter gunships, claiming a T-55 and a lorry in the process. In the face of such overwhelming firepower it was difficult to see how the Iraqi defences could possibly hold.

Once across the bridge things began to go rapidly wrong for the Marines as Iraqi RPGs forced the AAVs to scatter and 200 marines were pinned down for more than three hours. The tanks moved to clear the surrounding houses, but the AAVs proved vulnerable. One took two RPG rounds before a third finished it off. Four AAVs also became stuck in the mud along the Euphrates and came under fire. It was a sobering lesson for any marine who had thought that the crossing would be a 'walk in the park'.

On 26 March 2003, the Marines suffered sixty wounded and lost fifteen vehicles trying to reach the first bridge. They did not cross the second bridge until mid-afternoon. Even then the Iraqis were not prepared to concede defeat. Artillery had to be used to break up a concentration of about 1,000 Iraqi troops gathering at the city's train depot for a counter-attack. The following day, the Marines moved west to take a military barracks and the third bridge, which was secured by two tanks and three AAVs.

The US 7th Cavalry were engaged by Iraqi irregular forces firing RPGs and anti-tank guns near the city of An Najaf on 25 March. Despite the bad weather conditions the Americans succeeded in destroying more than thirty Iraqi vehicles. In Najaf itself the US 101st Airborne made repeated incursions to root out the remnants of regular and irregular Iraqi forces. Again near the city, a column of American tanks and APCs fought a skirmish, with a ragged force firing at them from an escapement. At Kut the US Marines also destroyed ten tanks and fourteen anti-aircraft guns.

Further west, during the initial push into Iraq, Abrams of Charlie Company, US 3rd Infantry Division, came up against Iraqi armour. This reportedly included T-72s, but most of the resistance was light, allowing them to press on swiftly. American helicopter gunships were reported to be attacking Republican Guard positions near the city of Karbala, south of Baghdad, on 24 March. They also received the attentions of America's giant B-52 bombers, which left a trail of death and destruction.

Pushing through the Karbala Gap, the Americans attacked the Medina Republican Guard Division just 113km south-west of Baghdad. The Iraqi force had been subject to continual Apache helicopter gunship and A-10 tank buster attack, and on 28 March airstrikes claimed four Iraqi tanks, six APCs and fifteen other vehicles.

To the Iraqi tank commanders it was evident that they had no freedom of movement and that the minute they did move, they were pounced on. Saddam was advised by his ground commanders that without support from the IrAF they were unable to mount any effective counter-attacks. More worrying was the morale of their men. Calls were made to the IrAF bases and promises made but nothing happened – Iraq's MiGs remained conspicuous by their absence.

The Medina's 10th Brigade collapsed on 3 April after two hours of air attack. According to a prisoner, his unit lost twenty-five tanks and two fuel lorries before fleeing back to Baghdad in their remaining trucks. Aided by the US 82nd Airborne, the

3rd Infantry took 2,500 prisoners on the road to Baghdad. Many had torn off their shoulder patches for fear the Americans would treat Republican Guards more harshly.

In a desperate attempt to stave off the American advance, those Republican Guard divisions around Baghdad (Hammurabi was dug-in to the south-west, Al Nida the south-east and Nebuchadnezzar to the north), despite a complete lack of air support, tried to engage them in open battle. They did little good. Saddam Hussein's supposedly elite Guard were attacked by US aircraft for the first time on 25 March 2003, as American ground troops encountered resistance to their advance on the capital. By the time the Americans had reached Baghdad they were claiming to have destroyed most of Iraq's 2,500-strong tank force.

For Saddam and his generals the situation was now rapidly disintegrating, as it was impossible to offer a coherent defence in the face of the US armoured columns. In the most notable advance, more than seventy Abrams and sixty Bradleys from the US 3rd Infantry's 2nd Brigade raced 370km in forty hours to take positions less than a day from Baghdad. On the night of 3/4 April, about 1,000 troops with armour support attacked Republican Guard and militiamen equipped with twenty tanks defending Saddam International Airport (SIA), just 19km to the west of Baghdad. En route to the airport, artillery and airstrikes crushed sporadic resistance. A-10 Thunderbolts reduced many Iraqi tanks to burning hulks, their crews having long fled.

One of the Republican Guard units, who were veterans of the fighting at Najaf, were thrown into the fighting as soon as it arrived in the Baghdad area on 4 April. The defenders of SIA bravely counter-attacked, losing 320 men, five tanks, three APCs, twenty-three trucks and more than thirty pieces of anti-aircraft artillery. In total, the Iraqis lost up to 600 soldiers killed in and around the airport.

The Iraqi government resolutely refused to acknowledge the loss of the airport, claiming to have thrown back the Americans after destroying eleven US tanks and eight APCs. Although expelled Iraqi forces and tanks continued to shell US positions within the airport they were quickly silenced by airstrikes. American warplanes destroyed a Special Republican Guard complex on the eastern side of the airport with missiles and laser guided bombs.

While helicopter-borne troops of the US 101st Airborne moved north of Baghdad, the road to Tikrit, Saddam's home town, was cut by US Special Forces. To the south, the US 1st Marine Division, having destroyed the Baghdad Republican Guard Division and seized Numaniyah Air Base, was closing in. To the south-east, having brushed aside Guard forces at Al Kut, the 1st Marine Expeditionary Force was also heading north.

By now the Iraqi command was in a state of panic, with many officers cut off from each other and unaware of what was happening on their flanks. The Nida Republican

Guard Armoured Division was reported no longer combat effective and the Adnan Division around Tikrit was targeted for further Coalition airstrikes. Some Republican Guard and regular army troops pulled back to an inner ring of defences around Baghdad to avoid being outflanked. In an attempt to shelter from the ever-present fighter-bombers Iraqi armour was deployed in the streets of Baghdad for the first time since the war began.

Some twenty-six Abrams and ten Bradleys swept into the city on 4 April on Operation Thunder Run, cutting it in two. They came within 3km of Saddam's bunker before swinging east to link up with US forces at the airport, leaving behind thirty knocked-out T-72s and 1,000 dead Republican Guard. Many of the Iraqi tanks, hidden in the side streets, were hunted down by British and American Special Forces, who called in pinpoint airstrikes using laser designators. However, up to fourteen tanks were witnessed intact near a southern flyover.

US military officials said twenty-five Abrams tanks and twelve Bradley armoured vehicles entered the Dawra suburb on a 'tour' from the airport during daylight hours on 5 April. The convoy met some resistance and returned to the airport. 'Republican Guard units around Baghdad have been crippled as an organized force,' stated General Moseley, USAF commander, adding, 'The Iraqi military as an organized defence in large combat formations doesn't really exist anymore.'

On the road to Baghdad at least sixty burnt-out Iraqi tanks and APCs were seen destroyed on 6 April. More than a dozen Iraqi tanks and APCs were knocked out near the main highway. The following day, as many as seventy Abrams and sixty Bradleys rolled into the Iraqi capital, supported by A-10s. The attack on Saddam's main presidential palace on the eastern banks of the Tigris took the defenders completely by surprise. American fire pounded Iraqi positions as they moved into the compound; the Bradleys did not even bother to move from the main exposed boulevard, catching the defenders in the rear. Most simply fled.

On 7 April, General Myers, Chairman, US Joint Chiefs of Staff, noted that of the 800-odd tanks the Republican Guard had started with, all but a couple of dozen had been destroyed or abandoned. By 8 April, four Abrams were operating from the compound of the presidential palace, and were involved in fierce exchanges. Abrams also moved onto the strategic Jumhuriya Bridge across the river Tigris and opened fire at targets in eastern Baghdad, while Apache helicopters attacked a Republican Guard compound.

Elsewhere, the 1st Marine Expeditionary Force continued its attack near Amarah, where the Marines met minimal resistance from the Iraqi 10th and 14th divisions. Most had already abandoned their weapons and fled after a period of air attack. On 8 April, US Marines from Task Force Tarawa moved to secure the headquarters of the Iraqi 10th Armoured Division at Amarah, a nearby airfield and an ammunition supply depot. They encountered no firing and received assistance from the locals, uncovering fifteen abandoned tanks and an assortment of weapons. Much of the 10th Division's armour was inoperable, having been left in earth positions as decoys. Using C-17 aircraft, American armour was also airlifted to the Haditha Dam area.

Nonetheless, the main focus continued to be the Iraqi capital. The 1st Marine Expeditionary Force then attacked across the Biyala River into the south-east corner of Baghdad, encountering T-72 tanks, APCs, surface-to-surface missiles, artillery pieces and numerous 'technical' vehicles (trucks with guns). They proceeded to seize Rashid Air Base, east of Baghdad. On 10 April, the Americans moved unopposed into the city centre, heralding the end of Saddam's regime. The Americans were greeted by cheering Iraqis, a moment clearly marking the end of organized resistance in Iraq.

The Special Republican Guard and the Adnan Republican Guard Division were expected to make a last stand at Tikrit, but after seven days of bombing the Americans brushed aside the 2,500 defenders. North of the city, the Iraqi troops fled their barracks, abandoning row upon row of armoured vehicles, including Chinese and Russian-built APCs. Some 250 US Marine armoured vehicles entered Tikrit on 13 April, passing at least five Iraqi tanks destroyed on the outskirts. Saddam's rule lay in tatters.

By now it was largely a case of mopping up. In western Iraq, the Iraqi 12th Armoured Brigade, defending the main road leading from Jordan to Baghdad, surrendered on 15 April at Ramadi to elements of the US 3rd Infantry. The newly arrived US 4th Infantry Division also fought a brief firefight near Taji Airfield, north of Baghdad, destroying a number of T-72s.

From the very start the Iraqis lacked the freedom of manoeuvre due to Coalition air supremacy. This meant they could show little initiative or offensive spirit. The regular army put up ad hoc resistance and in the south there was little organized activity by the Iraqi 11th Infantry Division, 6th Armoured Division and 51st Mechanized Division apart from the latter's foolish forays out of Basra. In fact, most of the fighting seemed to be conducted by Iraqi militia and Republican Guard.

It is notable that Iraqi tanks initially encountered on the road to Baghdad were ancient T-55s, then T-62s. It was not until the Coalition had almost reached the capital that the Iraqis threw in the Republican Guard's T-72s, by which time it was too late for them to make any difference. A captured Republican Guard colonel noted, 'From the beginning, I think that the balance of the air power is not equal. … The aircraft … destroyed our tanks and equipment.' In 1991 the Republican Guard were considered the key to Iraq's defence. Then they made a credible fighting withdrawal in 2003, equipped with obsolete armour and demoralized by the bombing, they just melted away.

When US armour rolled into Iraq its goal was Baghdad and the capture of Saddam Hussein.

A USMC M1A1 Abrams unleashes its 120mm gun on Iraqi forces fighting at Umm Qasr.

A Chinese-built Type 69 belonging to the Iraqi Army burning on Highway 27 on 2 April 2003.

An abandoned Iraqi MT-LB on the road north (see lower image, page 9).

Although outgunned, the Iraqis had superiority in numbers. This M1A1 was photographed burnt out on 5 April 2003 on Route 1.

The USMC Amphibious Assault Vehicle also suffered at the hands of the Iraqis crossing the Euphrates in late March.

Bradleys served with the US 3rd Infantry Division in the opening attack, which thrust toward Karbala.

A USMC gun crew firing in support of the attack; Iraqi defences had already sustained air strikes.

Iraqi armour struggled to concentrate for counter-attacks as they came under air attack before they could move into position. These abandoned Iraqi T-54/55 or Type 59/69 are west of Diwaniyah. The two vehicles in the background appear to be T-55 armoured recovery vehicles.

US Marine light armoured vehicles, based on the Swiss MOWAG 8x8 Piranha, pass through a US military checkpoint. This appears to be the version fitted with an Emerson twin TOW anti-tank missile launcher.

This Republican Guard T-72 Babylon Lion was apparently abandoned intact on the road to Baghdad.

It took American armoured columns just sixteen days to reach Baghdad in the face of varying levels of resistance.

Abandoned Iraqi T-72 and T-62 tanks gathered outside Baghdad covered in American graffiti; lacking freedom of manoeuvre, they proved easy prey.

Abrams of the US 1st Armored Division driving through Saddam Hussein's Hand of Victory monument.

A Bradley firing its 25mm chain gun. With the capture of Baghdad resistance did not end immediately.

The crew of an M2A3 Bradley take a break from the fighting – the boxes on the front are ERA, or explosive reactive armour.

This Bradley is on the streets of Sadr City, which forms part of Baghdad.

Soldiers from the US 3rd Infantry Division take cover by a M113 APC.

M3A3 Bradleys guarding a roadblock at Tikrit, Saddam Hussein's home town. It was thought he might make a dramatic last stand there, but instead, he fled.

This gunner is keeping an eye out for trouble in the far north of Iraq.

Like the British Defender and Snatch Land Rover, the unarmoured version of the HMMWV was to prove highly vulnerable in Iraq.

This US armoured dozer is shunting rubble from one of the roads into Baghdad. The concern was that such debris could be used to conceal improvised explosive devices.

A Bradley crew remain vigilant for sudden attacks by Saddam loyalists and other insurgents. Opportunist attacks using rocket-propelled grenades or home-made mines posed a particular threat.

Chapter Five

Where's Saddam's Air Force?

In the summer of 2002 Iraqi General Shalah had claimed categorically: 'Our air force's fighters are ready to confront and defeat the aggressors if they dare to approach our territories.' Nevertheless, Iraqi MiG-29s shooting down Coalition unmanned aerial vehicles was one thing; taking on the latest American air superiority fighters was another. The Coalition made it very clear, when more than 100 aircraft attacked Iraq's H3 Air Base in September 2002, that if the IrAF resisted it would be destroyed. Officially, the raid was part of the enforcement of the southern no-fly zone; in reality, it was placing a calling card that the IrAF could not fail to miss.

After that, Washington secretly put out feelers to individual IrAF commanders advising them not to resist. Replies came back to the effect that they might indeed prefer the alternative. The senior IrAF leadership comprised: General Hamid Rajah Shalah, IrAF Commander; General Saad Ahmad Naji, Assistant for Operations; General Ibrahim Ali Youssef, Commander of Aviation; General Sabah Mutlik, Commander of Training; and General Hussein Zibin, Commander IrAF Intelligence (though in 2002 he was believed to be the Iraqi Army Aviation Corps' commander).

Publicly, US Central Command, based in Doha, made it clear that it would attack all Iraqi aircraft, not only to prevent them from flying combat missions but also to prevent the delivery of WMD and the escape of the regime leadership. The Iraqis soon appreciated that nowhere was safe, except, it seems, Al Asad. To make it appear the IrAF was being torn apart, in early 2003 CENTCOM issued imagery of the attacks, but in reality the aircraft being blown up were ancient British-supplied Hunters and Soviet-supplied MiG-17s. On 4 April 2003, a solitary aircraft located near Al Taqqadum (also spelt al-Takatam) Airfield, west of Baghdad, was struck. Also in early April, elderly Iraqi MiG-21s, probably inoperable, parked in a revetment in the vicinity of Ramadi, were also hit. Where were the newer MiG-29, MiG-25 and Su-25 fighters?

Air bases and hardened aircraft shelters (HAS) were systematically targeted, as were Iraq's air defence, command and control, and intelligence facilities. In the face of up to 1,400 Coalition sorties a day, none of Iraq's armed forces showed much initiative. Coalition psychological operations (PSYOPS) included dropping more than 40 million leaflets prior to and during the conflict itself, urging the Iraqi people not to resist or face the consequences. CENTCOM was quick to illustrate its strategy, reporting HAS destroyed near Karbala, while in late March, F-14s dropped precision-guided munitions on the hangars at Al Taqqadum. It was allegedly the largest and most important fighter base the Iraqi Air Force had. The US Department of Defense (DoD) also showed F/A-18s dropping precision-guided missiles on Al Taqaddum, damaging the runways and taxiways, noting that there had been no Iraqi aircraft activity.

The Iraqi Air Defence Command was not spared either. Although Saddam was assessed to have given the IrADC preferential treatment in terms of resources, it was widely believed that its surface-to-air missiles, anti-aircraft artillery, radars and support systems were in such disrepair and so out-of-date that they were unable to prevent American and British combat air patrols over the no-fly zones. However, continuing attacks on Coalition aircraft in these zones proved the IrADC was still very active. On 26 March 2003, nine SAM sites were attacked in downtown Baghdad and, on 1 April, an F-15 dropped a PGM on a suspected SA-2 missile site south-west of Karbala. Missile maintenance facilities were also hit, such as the facility in Mosul, believed to service all types of missiles, from short-range ballistic to air-to-air.

American RQ-1A Predator UAVs (unmanned aerial vehicles), stripped of their sensor systems, were used to draw SAM radar attention for subsequent targeting by Coalition suppression of enemy air defence (SEAD) operations. Initially the IrADC put up quite a spirited fight over Baghdad. One American EA-6B Prowler pilot, conducting SEAD, experienced being shot at by up to seven SAMs all at once. This barrage, though, was largely ineffectual and there were claims that the poorly maintained Iraqi SAMs were falling back onto the city's civilian areas.

Iraqi air defences gave thirty-five AH-64D Apache Longbow helicopter gunships of the US 11th Aviation Regiment a surprise when they were attacking elements of the Republican Guard's Medina Division. The Iraqis resorted to that old, tried and tested expedient of human intelligence (HUMINT). On 24 March, an Iraqi major general in Najaf reported the location of the Apaches' assembly areas, and the fact they were on the move, to IrADC personnel using a cellular telephone. As a result the Apaches came under intense ground fire and lost a helicopter. This success was short-lived for the area was soon subject to intense attack by American A-10 Thunderbolts and British Harrier GR7s.

The Iraqi Army Air Corps was also singled out for special treatment, even if, like so much of the degraded Iraqi armed forces, it only posed a residual threat. In early 2003, the IrAAC, based at Al-Jadida, Baghdad, with air wings at Amarah, Basra, Iskandarya and Taji, was subjected to intense air attack. It was assessed that out of a fleet of 500 helicopters, probably less than 50 per cent were operational. Even this was much too optimistic. The Iraqis made concerted attempts to keep their attack helicopter fleet airworthy but it is hard to imagine more than fifty of its Mi-24, Gazelles and BO-105s combined were operational, and these were quickly destroyed on the ground.

Just two days into the ground war, on 22 March CENTCOM noted that the regime continued to move aircraft around on the ground in an effort to husband them. On 24 March, CENTCOM briefed that a MiG jet fighter had been towed away from the Al Asad airfield and hidden in a revetted area, and that Iraqi MiG-23 fighters had been dispersed to a cemetery near Balad airfield, north of Baghdad. CENTCOM even saw MiG fighters being buried – at Al Taqqadum, but interestingly made no mention of airstrikes on Al Asad.

Some of the IrAF's dispersal sites were seized within the first forty-eight hours. British and Australian SAS were used to secure the air bases known as H2 (with a runway of 12,795 feet) and H3 (the sector operations/interceptor centre with a runway of 10,000 feet), and three other airfields of a similar size in Iraq's western desert. Iraqi aircraft dispersed on H2 were then destroyed on the ground by American AC-130 gunships called in by the Special Forces.

From H2, Coalition Special Forces went Scud missile hunting – though none were found apart from two Al-Samoud missiles located near Hillah – and they directed aircraft, principally A-10 tank busters, against ground targets to the west and south of the airfield. Similarly, the air defence radar in the Western Desert near H3 was targeted by Coalition bombers. Mudaysis airfield, also in western Iraq, was targeted when an F-16 put a PGM onto its radar site. By late March, the Coalition was staging air operations from a number of Iraqi airfields under its control, Tallil, outside Nasiriyah, being the first.

While the Coalition quickly acknowledged air supremacy, it only put it at 95 per cent because of the IrADC's extensive stocks of AAA and SAMs. Lieutenant General Michael Moseley, Coalition Forces Air Component Commander, noted on April 5:

> His [Saddam's] air force in some aspects is still there. His airfields, for the most part, are not flyable. This morning we had only a handful of landing surfaces that could be used, and as we go through the day we will crater those again, as we do every day, to attempt to minimize any opportunity for him to fly.
>
> He has not flown to date. Of course we've killed a lot of his airplanes on the ground. We've broke up a lot of his command and control. We've attacked his military airfields and his air sustainment pieces, maintenance hangars and fuel and munitions, command and control on the bases.

Mosley declined to give a sense of what percentage of the Iraqi Air Force aircraft had been destroyed, but pointed out that the Coalition was alert to the Iraqis' frantic dispersal efforts. What he did not mention was the safe haven established at Al Asad.

Ironically, IrAF dispersal was rendered largely nugatory by the rapidity with which their air bases were overrun. One of the first to fall was Tallil, the sector/interceptor operations centre, after the garrison withdrew. Its two long runways, twin taxiways and three large ramp areas were taken intact. Despite a lot of unexploded ordnance and local militia still in the area it was soon up and running for the US 392nd Air Expeditionary Group. British operations in the south quickly neutralized Az Zubayr Air Base, near Basra. The American thrust north ensured that Karbala Northeast (a civilian site) and the military facilities at Habbaniyah and Baghdad Muthenna were non-viable. By 1 May 2003, the Habbaniyah area was occupied.

When US Marines overwhelmed the Iraqi forces defending SIA, just 8km to the west of Baghdad, on 3-4 April, they shot up the civilian aircraft, mostly already wrecked, lying on the runway. The facility was both military and civilian and the Marines made themselves at home in the airport's HAS, which contained nothing but thin air. The US 58th Aviation Regiment soon had the control tower up and running and the airport was symbolically renamed Baghdad International.

To the south of the capital, US Marines, having destroyed the Baghdad Republican Guard Division, seized Numaniyah Air Base. To the east of Baghdad, American forces expected to find the vast Rashid Air Base stiffly defended by IrAF personnel, Special Republican Guard and Republican Guard. Notably, Rashid was home to the Republican Guard and Special Transport squadrons. Instead they entered the facility without facing any real resistance. Of the IrAF there was no sign; once again, they had fled.

US Marines secured Amarah Air Base and interceptor operations centre on 8 April. Three days later, American forces entered Tikrit, securing Al Bakr Air Base (home to MiG-23, Su-24, Su-22 and various transport squadrons) and Tikrit East and South (both with 10,000ft military runways). The war for the IrAF was all but over, though resistance continued at some IrAF facilities. In mid-April, the newly arrived US 4th Infantry Division fought a brief firefight near Al-Taji airfield, north of Baghdad. By 16 April, the Americans also had control of Samarra, thereby securing the military air base at Samarra East.

General Saadoun was taken at Rashid Air Base and Lieutenant General Muzahim Sa'b Hassan al-Tikriti fell into American hands at the end of the month. The capture of the IrAF's commander, Hamid Raja Shalah al-Tikriti, was announced on 14 June 2003. The fate of the other IrAF generals was not made public; CENTCOM and the Combined Joint Task Force-7 in Baghdad, tasked with hunting the Iraqi senior leadership, declined to comment on their whereabouts. As early as 7 April, a US

Hercules transport aircraft is believed to have evacuated senior Iraqi military officials from Baghdad who had co-operated with the invasion.

What happened to those Iraqi aircraft that survived or were spared the bombing? Coalition Special Forces soon discovered Iraq's concealed hardware. After the wake-up call attack on the H3 Air Base, the Iraqi Fighter Command base at Al Asad had kept its head down. On 16 April 2003, it was swiftly secured by the Australian SAS in the face of very light resistance.

An initial count showed fifteen intact Iraqi aircraft. This grew to fifty-one, including MiG-25s, as well as 80,000 tonnes of explosives, which had clearly been spared by the Americans. Some aircraft were under camouflage netting beneath the palms and others were buried or concealed in nearby riverbeds. Not one bomb had fallen on the air base. The Australian SAS brigadier in charge made it apparent that the IrAF had been secretly offered a way out, and they had taken it.

Additionally, despite the airstrikes at Al Taqqadum, the Americans discovered buried in up to 30 feet of sand about thirty MiG and Sukhoi fighters wrapped in plastic sheeting. Amongst those dug up was a MiG-25RBT, an electronic intelligence-gathering variant dating from 1978-82. Along Highway 1, the road that runs north of Tikrit, Coalition forces discovered five small aeroplanes covered with camouflage. These were destroyed to prevent their use by the regime leaders. Six VIP helicopters were also found near the Ba'ath Party headquarters in Baghdad.

It seems that around 50 per cent of the aircraft originally assessed to be operational was recovered – perhaps some 50-80 fighters. The newer and better condition aircraft, such as the MiG-29 and MiG-25, were swiftly dispatched to America's National Air & Space Intelligence Centre (NIAC). This is USAF's main scientific exploitation centre, located at Wright-Patterson, AFB, Ohio. NIAC is responsible for assessing foreign aerospace capabilities and examined Iraqi MiG-29 in the wake of Desert Storm. The US Army also took samples for exploitation. For example, Iraqi BO-105C helicopters cropped up at Biggs Army Airfield (Fort Bliss), in Texas.

Saddam's largely ineffectual air defences also soon came to light. Numerous air defence weapons were unearthed in Baghdad, including partially destroyed Russian SA-7 man-portable SAMs. Coalition forces found SAMs, along with the VIP helicopters, near the Ba'ath Party HQ in Baghdad on 14 April. US Marines also discovered a truckload of SA-6 SAMs south-east of Baghdad. At the end of the first week of April, the 101st Airborne Division located an underground storage facility containing Roland air defence missiles near the town of Karbala.

The Coalition discovered Iraqi air defences cynically placed in civilian sites to deter air attack. For example, in Baghdad an Iraqi artillery unit, with ammunition placed at various points, was deployed in a park in the middle of a residential neighbourhood across the street from a girls' school. It was apparent that the Iraqis would fire a gun, move it, fire again, and continue the process as a way of avoiding being bombed. In Kut, more than twenty anti-aircraft guns were removed by the US Marines from an amusement park.

The no-show by the IrAF made Coalition air and ground operations much easier. However, the IrAF's acquiescence to the invasion backfired. They received a blow in mid-2003, when it was announced the old 400,000-strong Iraqi armed forces would be disbanded and replaced by the Iraqi Civil Defence Corps (ICDC), which would not include an air force.

The Iraqi air and air defence forces had no answer to the US carrier task groups stationed in the Gulf. These USN F/A-18 Hornet strike aircraft are flying in support of Operation Iraqi Freedom in late January 2003.

Photographed in late March, this RAF Tornado is subjected to a blinding sandstorm at an unspecified air base in the Middle East.

RAF ground crew prepare an AGM-65 Maverick laser-guided air-to-ground missile, which was designed for close air support.

Two US F-16 Fighting Falcons dropping decoy flares over Iraq. Suppression of air defence missions ensured that most Iraqi air bases and missile and radar sites had been put out of action before the ground war started.

What remained of Saddam's Air Force was persuaded not to fight. While Iraq had considerable air defences, much of it was obsolete, such as the anti-aircraft gun found in an Iraqi car park.

British Lynxes on 21 March 2003. These flew ground support and anti-tank missions. The launch rails are empty, indicating they are just returning from an operation.

An RAF GR4A Tornado armed with Storm Shadow missiles on 22 March 2003. The missiles are visible on the belly of the aircraft.

A USN F/A-18 Hornet being launched from a carrier – American airpower was simply overwhelming.

The US Marine Corps also deployed its amphibious assault ships, which are essentially mini carriers, to the Gulf. This shot was taken on 25 April 2003 and shows a USMC AV-8 Harrier hovering over the USS *Bataan*.

The business end of a British Harrier jump jet. Its weapons pylons are loaded with various ordnance, which include Paveway laser-guided bombs ready for a combat mission.

The Iraqi Army Air Corps had some attack helicopters, such as the Mi-24 Hind. This one is an Iranian war trophy.

Another Tornado GR4 is readied for its next strike mission.

An RAF VC-10 refuelling two Tornado F3s. Note the missiles on their fuselage. Air-to-air refuelling greatly extended fighter-bombers' combat range and gave greater mission loitering time.

Chinooks carrying 105mm ammunition from HMS *Ocean*. Such heavy lifting was vital in keeping the Royal Marines resupplied once ashore.

The IrAF went to great lengths to hide their aircraft, as this exhumed MiG-25 testifies. The sand can only have played havoc with the avionics.

US forces digging up an Iraqi M-G-25RBT Foxbat in the summer of 2003 at Al Taqaddum, west of Baghdad. The Americans discovered thirty jet fighters buried at this base.

The MiG slowly emerges from its hiding place.

USN carrier based F-14B Tomcats on patrol over Iraq in July 2004. They were able to launch strike missions at very short notice.

Gazelle and Sea King helicopters operating from HMS *Ocean* during Operation Telic.

An RAF Tornado
on dawn patrol.

A member of the ordnance ground crew on the carrier USS *Harry S Truman* checks an AGM-65 Maverick loaded onto an F/A-18 Hornet just prior to a mission over Iraq, in late November 2004.

A USN F/A-18 Hornet on a combat mission over Iraq in late March 2005 – the Coalition always enjoyed complete air supremacy.

This F-16 Fight Falcon was photographed over Iraq in June 2008.

Chapter Six

The Fate of Saddam's Navy

The tatty remains of Saddam Hussein's tiny naval forces finally ceased to exist at the end of March 2003. Their contribution to Saddam's resistance to Operation Iraqi Freedom was almost farcical, consisting of trying to lay mines in the Gulf, using little more than tug boats, and haphazzardly firing coastal defence missiles vaguely in the direction of Kuwait. The Coalition's fear that the Iraqis would deploy swarms of small boats armed with rocket-propelled grenades or even suicide craft, similar to the one used against the USS *Cole* off Aden in 2000, simply did not materialize.

In effect, Saddam's navy was the fleet that never was, even though his grandiose plans had been to rival the relatively powerful Iranian Navy. Fortunately, his scheme to create an effective, modern, surface combat force never came to fruition, being thwarted by the outbreak of the Iran-Iraq War and the subsequent 1991 Gulf War. During the latter, under constant attack, the small Iraqi fleet was all but wiped out and the vital naval base at Umm Qasr closed. In early 2003, as the UN's confrontation with Baghdad escalated, the remnants of the Iraqi Navy could only watch impotently the steady Western naval build-up in the northern Gulf.

Originally Moscow provided various patrol boats and fast Osa missile patrol craft, creating an effective fledgling Iraqi Navy based at Basra and at Umm Qasr. As far as Saddam was concerned the missile boats were just the start of things. His aspirations for his small fleet were revealed in early 1980, when he ordered ten warships, comprising four frigates and six corvettes, and a support ship from Italy worth $1.5 billion. However, none of them were ever delivered because of the Iran-Iraq War. In early March 2003, some of Iraq's Italian-built warships were still rusting away at Italy's La Spezia naval base. The Iraqi skeleton crew were awaiting a regime change that would finally allow them to go home.

Had Saddam contented himself with the Kuwaiti islands of Bubiyan, Warbah and part of the Rumaila oilfield in 1990, there is a good chance he would have got away with it like some thief in the night. The UN would probably not have acted in such a concerted manner beyond the imposition of punitive sanctions and he was already used to those. Such an outcome would have met his strategic, economic and, most importantly, naval needs. Instead, by occupying the whole of Kuwait, he unleashed a military response, the scale of which even he cannot have anticipated. Whilst the Iraqi Army and Air Force survived to fight another day, the Iraqi Navy did not. In many ways it was Saddam's strategic naval ambitions that led to the two previous wars, by clinging to his WMD ambitions, he led Iraq into a third.

The maelstrom of Desert Storm in 1991 largely finished off Iraq's fledgling navy. In the aftermath the naval base at Umm Qasr was declared part of a demilitarized zone along the Iraq-Kuwaiti border and all equipment was impounded. Although Saddam Hussein's sanction busting was highly effective in the 1990s, he only directed funds and equipment to his security apparatus and air defence forces; the navy got nothing.

By the late 1990s the Iraqi Navy was assessed to number just 2,500 personnel, equipped with an ancient training frigate and seven patrol and coastal combatants. At best this was little more than a coastguard with limited facilities at Basra and Khor Al-Zubair. Umm Qasr remained closed until 1998, when the United Nations Special Commission in Iraq (UNSCOM) were forced to leave by Iraqi non-compliance. However, the base's proximity to the Kuwaiti border meant it was very vulnerable.

From the very beginning of Operation Iraqi Freedom the Iraqi Navy knew that it could do little to withstand Coalition air strikes or indeed the attentions of the Special Forces. The Battle of Bubiyan Island in 1991 served to remind them just how powerless they were. Iraqi naval strategy consisted simply of obstructing Coalition access to Umm Qasr and Basra. The Iraqis' naval options were so limited that they resorted to that expedient of minelaying and, in an effort to avoid detection, used civilian vessels. Just as hostilities were opening on 19 March, there was a fracas between Iraqi divers operating from small boats that may have been attempting to lay mines and Kuwaiti naval forces.

Two days later, action against the Iraqi Navy heated up in the waters off Iraq's Al-Faw Peninsula. A US Navy P-3C Orion maritime patrol aircraft located an Iraqi patrol boat near some oil platforms, directed in an AC-130 gunship from USAF's 4th Special Operations Squadron, which quickly targeted the boat. Also that day an Iraqi tug carrying mines was seized in the northern Gulf, while at nightfall British naval forces sank two further Iraqi patrol boats that had foolishly ventured out to sea. Even if the Iraqis intended to disperse their boats, many were already non-operational and six were captured largely intact at Umm Qasr.

The symbolic coup de grace was delivered on 25 March when a Coalition raid hit the naval base at Basra, targeting two large patrol boats and a supply ship. Also struck was the *Al Mansur*, Saddam Hussein's luxury yacht, eight decks high, with helicopter pad and glass-domed atrium. It appeared to have suffered a direct hit and was left burnt and twisted, its superstructure partly torn off. Ironically, despite having no military value, other than as a 'prestige' target, it was the largest ship in the Iraqi Navy. This left one patrol boat and a number of small 'suicide' speedboats at large.

Iraqi attempts at minelaying were short-lived after Australian naval forces intercepted and boarded three Iraqi tugs and a barge containing nearly 100 ancient mines in the Khor Abd Allah Waterway; the tug *Jumariya,* towing a barge with twenty Manta and forty-eight LUGM mines; the tug *Al Raya,* with eighteen LUGM mines; and Tug 0, with no mines but had a minimal crew carrying uniforms and small arms. The vessels were using rows of oil drums to conceal the mines.

Despite this success, on 27 March there were two separate explosions by possible mines in the Khawr Abd Allah. Additionally, the presence of mines and sunken Iraqi vessels in the channel leading from Umm Qasr to the Gulf delayed British humanitarian aid.

Despite the destruction of the Iraqi Navy and the clearing of Iraqi mines, Iraqi forces continued to contest their waterways. On 30 March, Iraqis equipped with small arms and RPGs ambushed two Royal Marine launches on the river Zubayr just south of Crossing Point Bella, a vital bridge on the Al-Faw Peninsula. The boats had been supporting Operation James, designed to secure Abu al Khasib, a suburb a few kilometres to the south-west of Basra. Further south, British Royal Marines sallying up the Shatt al-Basra Waterway blew up three Iraqi gunboats.

This all but signalled the Iraqi Navy's final and futile contribution to resisting the Coalition. When the British finally secured Basra naval base in early April they found that the remnants of the Iraqi Navy still afloat consisted of a grey tug boat armed with a twin 57mm. The obliteration of Saddam's navy was complete.

In the face of the US and British fleets Iraq could do little to counter Coalition naval forces in the Gulf. The tiny Iraqi Navy was unable to protect Al Faw, Umm Qasr or Basra.

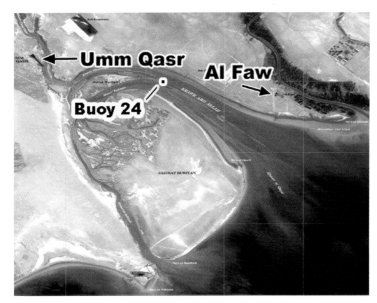

The southern approaches to Basra showing Bubiyan Island and Umm Qasr at the entrance to the Shatt al-Arab Waterway.

Coalition air strikes targeted any Iraqi naval assets, including Saddam's luxury yacht, the *Al Mansur*, seen here.

Mines were the greatest hazard to Coalition vessels. This Iraqi tug was concealing a particularly deadly cargo.

Likewise, this launch was used for mine laying.

The apparently innocent cargo stowed on an Iraqi tug – sections of oil drums were used to disguise mines to great effect.

A US EOD expert takes a closer look at a captured Iraqi mine.

Had these LUGM mines gone into the water they could have caused havoc.

Members of the Royal Regiment of Fusiliers guard an old Soviet-designed Silkworm/Styx anti-ship missile found in the Al Ma Qil area of Basra on its launcher in travelling configuration. EOD specialists soon found that it had no warhead.

Iraqi civilians fraternize with their 'liberators' in the Iraqi port of Umm Qasr.

Humanitarian aid being unloaded at Umm Qasr. This process was delayed by Iraq mines and sunken vessels.

HMS *Sandown* conducting mine clearance off Umm Qasr, supported by an Australian Sea King.

A British Lynx from 847 Naval Air Squadron on patrol over the clear, shallow waters of the Gulf.

Chapter Seven

A Tarnished Reputation

In light of the remarkable success of Desert Storm, armoured warfare analysts scrutinized the invasion of Iraq in early 2003 very closely. Extensive fighting in built-up areas against lightly armed irregular forces highlighted the shortcomings of a number of armoured systems. Additionally, endemic accidents, with vehicles falling into canals, ravines, running into powers lines, and rear-ending each other, resulted in continuing and unnecessary non-combatant fatalities.

In the wake of Operation Iraqi Freedom the US Department of Defense (DoD) and America's armoured vehicle manufacturers issued initial findings about the performance of their military vehicles during the invasion. Alarmingly, the Arab media claimed that America and Britain lost seventy tanks and more than 400 other vehicles. Whilst this is a gross exaggeration, much to the concern of DoD and General Dynamics Land Systems (GDLS), the M1A1/2 Abrams certainly tarnished its reputation.

Once the dust began to settle it seemed that US armoured vehicles had not been as overwhelming as initially thought. The American M1A1, which was deployed to the Gulf in 1991, had since been supplemented by the A2 variant (both as an upgrade and as a new build), which notably provides greatly enhanced survivability capabilities and is equipped with a whole new generation of ammunition. Keen attention was paid to how these enhancements performed.

A report issued by America's Tank and Automotive Command (TACOM) painted a less than rosy picture of the performance of the US Marines M1A1s. During the whole of Desert Storm, of the 1,955 M1A1 tanks in theatre, quite remarkably only four were disabled and four damaged but repairable. This was not bad going considering there were a number of battles against the Iraqi Republican Guard's T-72 tanks.

In 2003 the fighting was much more close quarter and reportedly sixteen M1A1 Abrams were damaged or destroyed, which was worrying as most of the resistance came from Iraqis armed with rocket-propelled grenades. It was anticipated that one of the biggest threats to the M1A1 would be the Soviet AT-14 Kornet anti-tank guided missile; Syria had provided Iraq with twelve launchers and 200 missiles in late

2002. However, most M1A1 losses were as a result of indirect hits by RPG-7/16, which often led to fires and the crews bailing out.

An RPG disabled an Abrams near Karbala after it penetrated the engine compartment. The Abrams' non-ballistic skirts were also penetrated by the RPG but this only caused cosmetic damage. At least three tanks were reported captured by the Iraqis near Karbala, presumably because they were abandoned after problems. Another tank had to be abandoned because of mechanical failure on the approach to Baghdad. It was hit from the rear and caught fire. The crew doused the flames and a second tank took it under tow. However, they eventually abandoned it, leaving the burnt hulk to be shown triumphantly on Iraqi television.

According to TACOM there were 'no catastrophic losses due to Iraqi direct or indirect fire', but a number of tanks were destroyed due to secondary effects attributed to Iraqi weapon systems. TACOM noted that the Abrams' top side and rear armour remained susceptible to penetration and needed improving. In Abrams defence, TACOM concluded: 'The tank performed extremely well, providing excellent manoeuvre, firepower and overall protection.' Most of the Iraqi RPGs just bounced off the Abrams and, as long as they had fuel, they were unstoppable on their drive to Baghdad.

According to the US Army, of the sixteen tanks lost, only two were actually destroyed and most losses were due to mechanical failure or disabled vehicles being vandalized by the Iraqis. Of those damaged, one may have been the result of friendly fire; an Abrams near Najaf was struck in the engine compartment by a 25mm armour-piercing depleted uranium round, presumably from a Bradley or a LAV-25. However, according to media sources the figures were actually much starker than the DoD let on: 151 M1s received hits from varying calibre weapons; three were destroyed and twelve were damaged beyond repair. The Iraqis also captured about half a dozen.

During the fighting, accidents were also commonplace. One Abrams fell off a bridge and sank without anyone noticing for several hours, while others got stuck in the mud. One 1st Marine Division Abrams was lost on 27 March 2003 when it fell into the river Euphrates during combat operations north-west of Nasiriyah. Unfortunately, Corporal Robert M. Rodriguez was drowned and his body was not retrieved until three days later. Similarly there were a number of friendly fire incidents. In one instance a USMC AH-1W SuperCobra attack helicopter hit an Abrams with a Hellfire missile at Basra.

Unfortunately, the US Marines amphibious assault vehicle 7A1 also proved to be susceptible to RPG rounds. The Marines assaulted the first bridge at Nasiriyah on 26 March 2003, with twenty AAVs, losing three quarters of their number. Casualties in AAVs continued. For example, on 7 April 2003 Lance Corporal Andrew Julian Aviles,

4th Marine Division, was killed in central Iraq when an enemy artillery round struck his vehicle. On the same day, Corporal Jesus Martin Antonio Medellin, 1st Marine Division, suffered a similar fate.

Some 2,200 Bradley infantry fighting vehicles were deployed in theatre in 1991, of which only three were reported disabled. After Desert Storm the US embarked a high-survivability Bradley Modification Plan and the M2/3A1s were upgraded to A2 standard to reflect the lessons learned. The latest Bradley's deployed to the Gulf were fitted with explosive reactive armour, which gives a greater degree of protection from high explosive anti-tank warheads such as the Russian RPG-7.

Media figures reported that sixteen IFVs were destroyed and thirty-five seriously damaged. The Bradley IFV, whilst fending off RPG rounds, was susceptible to unconventional attack. On 10 April 2003, a car bomb exploded next to a Bradley, claiming one of its crew. Four days later, another American soldier was killed in a friendly fire incident, after being struck by an armour-piercing round fired by an M2 Bradley. On 12 October 2003, James Powell, of the US 4th Infantry Division, was killed when his Bradley struck an enemy anti-tank mine. Accidents reportedly included one US 3rd Infantry Division Bradley rolling off a cliff. As well as the IFV losses, up to twenty-three armoured personnel carriers were also allegedly lost. One M113A3 was reported hit on 3 April and a M109A6 was apparently destroyed after a round misfired, causing the vehicle to burn out.

During Iraqi Freedom the US Army and USMC lost up to thirty Hummers and about twenty lorries, although some media sources claim that fifty lorries were lost. Once the Iraqi armed forces collapsed there were unending attacks and accidents involving the HMMWV. For example, on 17 April 2003, two soldiers were killed when an Iraqi grenade exploded inside their Hummer. On the same date, an American soldier was killed in Kuwait after his HMMWV turned over.

It is unclear what armour losses were like amongst the 2nd and 3rd Armored Cavalry regiments, 4th Infantry Division, during Operations Desert Scorpion, Peninsula Strike and Sidewinder conducted during June 2003 to mop up in Iraq. By late 2003, ambushes on American military columns were being reported with increasing frequency. While the Pentagon pored over the Abrams' shortcomings, it still made a remarkable contribution to getting US forces to Baghdad in just sixteen days. The Abrams' reputation may have been tarnished but it certainly had not lost all its Desert Storm lustre.

In 1991, no British Challenger 1s were lost to enemy action. Losses in 2003 amounted to one Challenger 2's turret and glacis damaged by friendly fire, which unfortunately resulted in two dead. A British Scimitar was also knocked out inadvertently by an American A-10 tank buster, mirroring the loss of a Warrior IFV in 1991.

In 2003 there was much more close-quarter combat than in the 1991 Gulf War and double the number of M1A1 Abrams were damaged. Shortcomings were soon discovered with most of the armoured vehicles deployed for Operation Iraqi Freedom.

US mechanics remove an Abrams' engine; most losses were due to rocket-propelled grenades, of which the Iraqis had considerable stocks.

Giving some indication of the level of Iraqi resistance, media sources claimed that, in total, 151 Abrams were hit, with three destroyed and twelve write-offs.

In total, sixteen US infantry fighting vehicles were destroyed and thirty-five damaged – the Bradley proved vulnerable to Iraqi car bombs, mines and IEDs.

APCs such as the M113 also suffered losses. The occupants often received impact injuries if the blast was sufficient to lift the vehicle.

During Operation Iraqi Freedom the Americans lost thirty HMMWVs, or Hummers. They were easy targets in the close confines of Iraq's cities.

Only one British Challenger 2 was damaged, and that was due to friendly fire. These two are providing fire support during the assault on Basra.

Unfortunately, a US A-10 tank buster destroyed a British Scimitar in a friendly fire incident. This one belonged to the Queen's Dragoon Guards.

Warriors belonging to the Black Watch Battle Group on low-loaders in southern Iraq. Armoured vehicles had to be moved long distance in this way to prevent damage to the tracks and running gear.

A Household Cavalry Regiment Scimitar on patrol with a 1 Para WMIK Land Rover outside Basra. The latter soon proved to be highly vulnerable in Iraq as it offered the crew no ballistic protection.

Likewise, the Snatch Land Rover was ill-equipped to cope with the escalating insurgency in Iraq and gave no protection from small-arms fire or IEDs.

In contrast, the M1114 up-armoured HMMWV offered some protection from small arms, mines and artillery fire, but it could not cope with the RPG. This vehicle is serving with the US 1st Armored Division in Taji.

Hummers of the US 1st Cavalry Division protecting Iraq's main power station. Insurgents soon set about wrecking the country's remaining infrastructure.

A convoy of Bradleys and Hummers in Taji in the summer of 2004. These vehicles look like they were straight off the factory floor.

M113s of the US 1st Armored Division on the streets of Sadr City in late 2004. This suburb of Baghdad soon became a hotbed of insurgency.

The British Challenger 2 performed well during Operation Telic.

Warriors of the Black Watch Battle Group. The air conditioning on these and other British vehicles proved a major headache as it kept breaking down.

Chapter Eight

Zarqawi's Storm

The success of Operation Iraqi Freedom was soon to have unforeseen and unwelcome consequences. Shattering Saddam's military with a knock-out blow proved to be the easy bit; putting Iraq back together again was an altogether different matter. Without the strong and brutal hand of Saddam it was not long before those with a vested interest in overturning the old status quo were competing for power.

Disastrously for Iraq, while Washington had a very clear military strategy for bringing down Saddam, it exhibited an appalling lack of foresight when it came to overseeing the transition to a post-Saddam regime. As American political commentator Kevin Phillips notes, 'The supposed liberation of Iraq in 2003 unleashed guerrilla warfare and produced a massive anti-American surge in Islamic nations from North Africa to Indonesia. One side effect may have been to print recruiting posters for a generation of suicide bombers.'

One of Operation Iraqi Freedom's fundamental flaws was that it was not backed up by an exile Iraqi government in waiting that could swiftly pick up the reins once Saddam and his Ba'ath Party stooges were thrown out. Unfortunately, the Americans reasoned most Iraqi exiles were former Saddam generals and officials and could not be trusted. Likewise, because Saddam's military and police were seen as tainted they were all sent home, with predictable results.

Following the invasion, looting across Iraq soon turned into organized attacks and the anarchy turned into insurgency in the Sunni central regions. Most of the militants were Iraqis who had offered the most resistance to the invasion in March and April – namely the Fedayeen, though they were soon to be reinforced by Islamists from other countries who made the most of Iraq's poorly guarded borders. The insurgency had all the hallmarks of the Palestinian Intifada: hit-and-run gunmen, car bombs and suicide bombers. It was particularly intense for the American forces in the Baghdad area known as the 'Sunni Triangle'.

Washington claimed that one of its key reasons for attacking Iraq was because of Saddam Hussein's links with al-Qaeda. This rationale was based on alleged contact between al-Qaeda and Iraqi intelligence in Afghanistan, Pakistan and Sudan during the early 1990s. In fact, initially the Iraqi insurgency was largely home-grown. From the very start, Saddam and his intelligence services had always planned to wage a terror campaign against any occupiers. After the 1998 Desert Fox bombing campaign Saddam sought to set up a guerrilla army that would oppose any occupation and form the core of a new underground government.

Money, not militant Islam, was what Saddam proposed to use as the driving force behind his planned underground opposition to the Coalition. His intelligence services were behind the Fedayeen Saddam militia, which provided the initial opposition once the Iraqi armed forces had collapsed in the face of the invasion. The Fedayeen offered $100 to anyone prepared to fire a rocket-propelled grenade at American troops, with a $5,000 bounty on every US soldier killed.

While Australia committed 2,000 troops to the invasion, nearly forty countries subsequently sent troops to support security duties and create the multinational force in Iraq. While Georgia, Italy, Spain and South Korea sent several thousand, in most cases these forces numbered just a few hundred and were gradually withdrawn as the security situation deteriorated and casualties and kidnappings mounted.

The multinational 'peacekeeping' force divided Iraq into six geographical regions (North, North Central, Western, Baghdad, Centre South and South East). Each area was assigned a multinational division, although none of these were anywhere near divisional strength. Multinational Division (South East) was created in mid-2003 and placed under British command. Multinational Division Centre South became operational that year but maintaining international troop commitments proved a major headache for Washington.

Under British command the Multinational Division (South East) comprised more than 13,000 soldiers (from the UK, Italy, Australia, Japan, Denmark, the Czech Republic, Lithuania, Norway, Portugal, the US, Norway and Romania), supported by the local Iraqi 10th Division, numbering about 9,000. These forces were responsible for the ongoing security operations in south-eastern Iraq, including the cities of Basra and An Nasiriyah.

In the meantime, Saddam's sons, Uday and Qusay, were killed after being discovered in a safe house in Mosul on 29 June 2003 by Task Force 20. This success was short-lived; as Iraq's cities spiralled into anarchy it took eight months to track down Saddam Hussein. Finally, on 13 December 2003, Task Force 121 and elements of the US 4th Infantry Division ran Saddam to ground. He was executed three years later.

Within two years, the insurgency was all but unmanageable. The city of Haditha proved a constant thorn in the US military's side as it sits astride the main highway from Syria and formed part of a network of towns in Al Anbar Province used by insurgents. There was growing concern that the insurgents were becoming ever more sophisticated and were receiving help from Iran, Hezbollah in the Lebanon and Syria.

Nevertheless, from the very beginning the insurgency had a very clear foreign fighter element. The bombing of the UN HQ in Baghdad on 19 August 2003 and of the Najaf Mosque on 29 August 2003 resulted in the US concentrating on Jordanian commander Abu Musab al-Zarqawi and his foreign fighter network. His strategy for 'al-Qaeda in-Iraq' was to provoke civil war between Iraq's Shia and Sunni populations in order to make the country ungovernable and drive the Americans out.

Initially, US authorities seemed confused over whether al-Qaeda or al-Qaeda-inspired fighters were playing a key role in the growing insurgency. President Bush, in his 20 January 2004 State of the Union message, said: 'These killers, joined by foreign terrorists, are a serious, continuing danger.' While the military agreed with US politicians that there was a foreign component to the post-Saddam insurgency, there were sharply differing views about how significant a part they were playing.

After the arrest of suspected Osama bin Laden aide Hassan Ghul in January 2004, Lieutenant General Ricardo Sanchez, commander of US forces in Iraq, commented that the arrest 'is pretty strong proof that al-Qaeda is trying to gain a foothold here to continue their murderous campaigns.' At the same time, he seemed to be contradicted by General John Abizaid, in charge of US Central Command, which directed operations in the Middle East. 'I am confident,' said Abizaid, 'that there is no flood of foreign fighters coming in [to Iraq].'

At their height the overall numbers of insurgents was put at about 5,000, of whom about 3,000 were estimated to be foreign volunteers. By late 2006 and early 2007, senior US officials considered al-Qaeda in-Iraq as the driving force behind the insurgency. Its membership was estimated to number anything from 5,000 to 10,000 men, making it the largest Sunni extremist group in Iraq.

President Bush instigated a counter-insurgency campaign in January 2007, developed by General David Petraeus and involving a massive US troop surge in Iraq. By early 2008 there were signs that al-Qaeda was withering following a mass defection of Sunni supporters to the US military. More than 80,000 Sunnis helped the local tribal groups' Concerned Local Citizens militias to eject al-Qaeda from western and northern Iraq.

Critics of the invasion contend that Saddam had no real links with al-Qaeda and that the invasion prompted al-Qaeda or pro al-Qaeda elements to move into Iraq to fight the US military. If this is true then clearly Washington's actions created new al-Qaeda followers within Iraq and beyond. Certainly the Sunni-Shia schism in Iraq ensured that the country was a fertile recruiting ground for al-Qaeda.

The more cynical argue that Washington overemphasized the al-Qaeda threat to bolster public support for the war, especially once US casualties began to mount. From the Pentagon's perspective, the invasion had the desired effect in that it was always better to fight Islamists abroad rather than await further attacks on the US homeland.

The last US combat brigade left Iraq on 19 August 2010, although about 50,000 personnel remained to assist with the 'transition' process. US troops were only involved in combat operations at the request of the Iraqi government or if they came under attack. By this stage about 3,500 American troops had been killed in action and 32,000 wounded. (The UK lost 136 KIA before withdrawing in May 2009.) Civilian deaths were put in excess of 100,000.

Despite the continuing violence, US combat operations in Iraq ceased. President Obama made America's withdrawal a presidential election pledge and troop numbers began decreasing once he took office in January 2009. Many questioned whether America's disengagement in Iraq was premature. While sectarian bloodshed was down from the appalling days of 2006-07, during mid-2010 attacks both on civilians and on the Iraqi security forces were escalating on a daily basis. The Islamic State of Iraq (an umbrella grouping of Sunni militants that includes al-Qaeda in-Iraq) was believed to be responsible and the bloodshed continued.

US 101st Airborne troops cornered and killed Saddam's sons, Qusay and Uday, on 22 July 2003 in the northern city of Mosul. These Hummers are armed with missiles and heavy machine guns.

The end of Saddam's sons after the building they were hiding in was peppered with fire.

An Abrams crew take a welcome breather at sunset – within a year of the conventional invasion of Iraq, Coalition forces would be facing a bitter insurgency.

US troops passing a blazing car bomb. The man in the foreground is equipped with the M4 carbine. Following the fall of Saddam, swathes of the country became blighted by anarchy first perpetrated by loyalists and then jihadists.

More US troops checking that these men are not insurgents and their car is not being used to transport weapons or explosives.

House clearances looking for Saddam loyalists took on an entirely different complexion once the insurgency was hijacked by jihadists. The country also spiralled into civil war as the Shia and Sunnis set about each other to settle old scores.

Foot patrols soon found themselves targeted by snipers and IEDs. This infantryman from the US 3rd Infantry Division is clearly not taking any chances.

The sign on the Hummer sums up the rapidly disintegrating security situation in Iraq; any civilian vehicle coming close would be deemed a threat and fired on.

The Desert Hawk surveillance drone was used to gather real-time intelligence on insurgents' activities.

Likewise, the Raven UAV served the same purpose in Iraq.

The Black Watch Battle Group deployed to Iraq in late 2004 to help with security in the Basra area and cover for US units redeployed to Fallujah.

Low-loaders moving the Black Watch's equipment into southern Iraq.

Black Watch Warrior ACVs being prepared for battle at Shaibah. They soon found themselves involved in the encircling operations at Fallujah.

A tense moment for a 40 Commando roadblock outside Basra in the summer of 2004. These patrols were designed to protect Iraq's pipelines from sabotage but such interference soon became resented by the local population.

Convoy escort duties also soon became dangerous. These marines are guarding shipping containers; such large targets were very tempting to the mounting insurgency.

This checkpoint is also operated by the Iraqi police, whose support for Coalition stabilization efforts was always suspect. Insurgents often used Iraqi police uniforms to overcome local security measures.

A US 3rd Infantry Division Bradley is parked menacingly at an intersection between Camp Liberty and Camp Victory in late March 2005. Even armoured vehicles such as this could be susceptible to IEDs made from 155mm shells, which would be capable of flipping it.

This US 82nd Airborne paratrooper keeps a wary eye on a passing Iraqi police car in Tal Afar in October 2005. Insurgents were known to pose as police in order to mount attacks.

These airborne troops and their Hummer are also on patrol in Tal Afar in early November 2005. Their task was to disrupt insurgent operations and seize weapons caches.

Marines from the US 2nd Marine Division on patrol in November 2005. The man on the right is carrying the M240 Squad Automatic Weapon or SAW. Their Hummer appears to have been converted into an open-topped troop carrier.

Military Police from the US 11th Armored Cavalry Regiment attend the site of a bomb attack on an Iraqi Police Station in Hamia in 2005. Note the different paint schemes, sand and olive drab, and weapons stations on the Hummers. Many ad hoc enhancements were conducted by the troops in the country.

After a car bomb exploded outside a police station in southern Baghdad on 17 April 2006, a second one was detonated to catch those responding to the first blast. There were eighteen casualties, including two policemen.

Chapter Nine

The Battle for Fallujah

Following the successful capture of Basra and Baghdad the Americans soon found themselves having to fight a series of bloody operations to pacify Iraq's restive cities. The city of Fallujah came to symbolize American complacency following the swift defeat of Saddam Hussein's armed forces. Having won the war so quickly, there remained the little matter of winning the peace. The Americans argued that the anarchy in the days following the capture of Baghdad was simply suppressed Iraqis letting off steam and everything would calm down of its own accord. This was wilful naivety in the extreme. Instead they made a major rod for their own and the rest of the Coalition's backs.

Fallujah lies to the west of Baghdad on the banks of the Euphrates and was known as the 'city of mosques', which numbered more than 200. Being a Sunni city it became one of Saddam Hussein's power bases and was in what the US military dubbed the Sunni Triangle. Airstrikes in 1991 – intended to cut the bridge over the Euphrates – resulted in the deaths of several hundred civilians. Following the invasion in 2003, the Iraqi military largely abandoned the city and it soon became unruly in the face of a US military presence.

The Americans knew that they had to draw a line in the sand in the face of the insurgents' growing gains across Iraq and make an example of Fallujah. All armies dislike conducting urban warfare so this was not a decision made lightly. It was when al-Qaeda in-Iraq's leader, al-Zarqawi, arrived in Fallujah that the Iraqi insurgency began to gather momentum and created a see-saw war on the streets of Iraq's main cities. The Americans came close to capturing him twice during 2003, but each time he escaped. His brutality was highlighted when he personally beheaded British engineer Kenneth Bigley in Fallujah in October 2004, an atrocity that, like many others, was posted on the Internet.

US troops were compelled to fight two major battles to pacify Fallujah in April and November 2004. The presence of al-Zarqawi and his supporters in Fallujah was a major headache for the US military. While his centre of operations was based in the city, with local Iraqi support, he was thought to have about 1,000 men – largely foreign fighters – in Iraq, particularly in Baghdad and Mosul. Initially, Fallujah had fallen under the influence of some 500 fighters, supported by about 2,000 part-timers. By the end of the year they had swelled to 3,000, making the city all but ungovernable.

Problems in Fallujah had simmered since 2003, when elements of the US 82nd Airborne Division moved into the city, and there had been a number of shooting incidents with the locals. This escalated, culminating in insurgents attacking a convoy carrying senior US generals in February 2004. The Americans first tried to secure the whole of Fallujah in early April 2004 with Operation Vigilant Resolve following the murder of four US contractors in the city and five soldiers in Habbaniyah. This involved surrounding Fallujah with several thousand troops to cut off the escape routes of the insurgents, followed by an assault by the US 1st Marine Expeditionary Force.

Some 3,600 men drawn from marine, army and airborne units were pitched against more than 2,000 insurgents. Arguably, the modest assault force, despite all its firepower, was simply not strong enough against a well-entrenched and determined enemy that knew every inch of the city. After three days of fighting the Marines only managed to secure a quarter of the city and mounting civilian casualties forced them to hold a unilateral ceasefire. The fighting then resumed until 1 May, when the Marines finally withdrew, handing their positions over to pro-Coalition Iraqi forces.

Notably, this initial battle marked the shift in conflict between the Coalition and Saddam regime loyalists to Islamist-inspired insurgents waging Jihad against Western infidels. It signalled to the insurgents that they could stand and fight against the might of the US military and prevail. This sent a very disturbing message across the rest of Iraq's troubled cities. The American withdrawal also meant the insurgents were able to turn the city into a militant stronghold.

At the same time, the Americans were battling for control of Ramadi, where about 300 insurgents had to be rooted out, most of whom were killed in the fighting. In early October, 5,000 American and Iraqi troops were also obliged to clear up to 1,000 supporters of al-Zarqawi from the city of Samarra.

The following month some 13,500 men gathered for an operation in Fallujah that included American, British and Iraqi troops – the bulk of them comprising 6,500 US marines and 1,500 US soldiers, along with 2,000 Iraqis. The British Army's Black Watch provided about 850 men to help with the encirclement operations that would cut the insurgents off from outside help. Units from the US 1st Cavalry Division and the Marines were also tasked with surrounding Fallujah. The insurgents knew an attack was coming because of the major Coalition troop build-up, plus the heavy artillery barrage and air attack.

The aptly named Operation Phantom Fury began on the night of 7 November 2004, when US and Iraq Special Forces moved to secure the outlying villages to the west of Fallujah and the city's general hospital. The Marines also moved to secure the Jurf Kas Sukr Bridge. US forces cut the electrical power to the city and then two US Marine regimental combat teams launched the assault to the north, assisted by units from the US 7th Cavalry Regiment and the 2nd Infantry Regiment (Mechanized). They were followed up by four infantry battalions.

Inside Fallujah the insurgents created a deadly rabbit warren of interlocking defences designed to funnel enemy forces into their fields of fire. They booby-trapped homes using massive IEDs (improvised explosive devices) built from oil drums and propane gas bottles, and any other explosives they could lay their hands on. Doors and windows were fitted with tripwires while roads and paths were sown with IEDs to catch the unwary. As well as mining them the insurgents blocked off roads using massive concrete barriers and blocked stairwells, creating rat runs in which to trap attacking troops. The concrete barriers were also used to make reinforced bunkers to withstand enemy fire. Mosques were converted into strongpoints and weapons depots. The net result was that up to a fifth of the city's buildings were destroyed and around half damaged as Coalition forces sought to winkle out the enemy fighters.

Within two days, by nightfall on 9 November, the Marines had pushed through to Highway 10 in the city centre. Although the fighting subsided by 13 November, sporadic but determined resistance continued for a number of days. Coalition forces suffered a total of 107 killed and 613 wounded during Operation Phantom Fury, while up to 2,000 insurgents were killed. The 2nd Battalion, US 2nd Infantry Regiment was awarded the Presidential Unit Citation for its actions during the battle.

It took the US Marines a total of nine days of tough street fighting in November 2004 to drive out the enemy, although the local insurgents stayed to fight. Ironically, as US troops were redeploying from Mosul to help at Fallujah, insurgents from Fallujah were filtering into Mosul. Remaining American forces in Mosul came under intense attack and the insurgents took over two-thirds of the city. Iraqi and US reinforcements had to be rushed in to wrestle back control.

The ferocity of the insurgency should not be underestimated. The Second Battle of Fallujah left 200,000 people displaced, 6,000 killed and thousands of buildings destroyed, including sixty mosques. American counter-insurgency tactics at this stage lacked subtlety; Abrams tanks, artillery and jets were used to blast insurgent strongholds at point-blank range. Once again, al-Zarqawi eluded his captors and he continued to campaign against Coalition forces, which he saw as infidels and foreign occupiers of Muslim land. The US military's victory was short-lived because, by September 2006, the whole of Al Anbar Province was in insurgent hands, with the exception of battered Fallujah. However, it would be another two years before the city was placed under the control of the Iraqi government.

As well as al-Qaeda-inspired Sunni insurgents in the Sunni Triangle, the Coalition also had to contend with Shia or Shi'ite militants. The latter were implacably opposed to the Sunnis and the Coalition. This in effect meant that Iraq was plunged into a three-way war. In the bloody aftermath of the 1991 Gulf War Iraqi Shia clerics fled to the Iranian city of Qom, the second holy city of Shia Islam. Khuzestan became home to more than 100,000 Iraqi Shia migrants. Mohammed Baqir al-Hakim's Badr Organization, part of the Supreme Council for Islamic Revolution in Iraq, was never short of recruits. However, following the 2003 invasion of Iraq, at Washington's invitation, al-Hakim, minus his Iranian-backed army, was allowed to return home to help form an interim Iraqi government.

In the meantime the Iraqi Shia Madhi Army came into being as a resistance movement intended to oppose what it saw as America's occupation, initially drawing on seminary students linked to Muqtada al-Sadr in Baghdad's Sadr City district, formerly Saddam City. They moved swiftly to fill the vacuum left by the collapse of Saddam's regime as the Coalition struggled to form a viable successor government. After three wars there was no shortage of weapons scattered across Iraq and in the wake of the Coalition's invasion many arms dumps were left unguarded. This meant that Shia and Sunni insurgents were easily able to lay their hands on small arms, support weapons and explosives.

Initially, al-Sadr held back from joining Saddam's Ba'athist guerrillas and Sunni Islamists, who were soon launching attacks on Coalition forces. In the meantime, the Mahdi Army's ranks swelled to 10,000-strong. Fuelling the flames of sectarian violence, on 29 August 2003 Mohammed Baqir al-Hakim, leader of the rival Shia Badr organization, was assassinated by a massive car bomb at the Imam Ali Mosque in Najaf. While the blame was laid on anti-Shia Sunnis, especially Saddam loyalists, in light of growing Shia rivalry the finger was also pointed at Muqtada al-Sadr. American intelligence blamed al-Qaeda in-Iraq's leader, Jordanian Sunni Abu Musab al-Zarqawi.

Things came to a head with the Shia in April 2004 after the authorities turned their attentions to al-Sadr's activities. In response, as well as taking control of Sadr City, the Mahdi Army launched a major offensive across Iraq. While the gunmen on the streets of cities such as Baghdad and Najaf were accredited to the Mahdi militia, in truth many were ordinary Iraqis forced to defend their neighbourhoods against spreading anarchy. The following month the Coalition sought to drive the Mahdi Army from southern Iraq and it withdrew from Karbala, though held on to the Najaf-Kuga region.

Following a ceasefire, hostilities broke out again that summer. Almost 4,000 American and Iraqi troops trapped 2,000 Mahdi militia in the Imam Ali shrine in Najaf. A tense three-week stand-off followed. During 2005, al-Sadr's supporters contested the Iraqi elections and the following year avoided armed confrontation with the Coalition and the Iraqi government. In return, no attempt was made to arrest al-Sadr or reassert control of those areas in southern Iraq held by the Mahdi.

By the summer of 2005, insurgents were attacking British forces in the southern

Amarah area with increasing sophistication. These predominantly Shia militants received not only Iranian help, but also support from Syria and Hezbollah. Because of Syria's long-standing support for Palestinian groups such as Hamas and Islamic Jihad, and Lebanon's Hezbollah, it became inevitable that Syria would be a conduit for Jihadists flowing into Iraq. The Lebanese group Hezbollah provided assistance in 2006.

According to US intelligence, up to 2,000 members of Muqtada al-Sadr's Mahdi Army and other Shia militias received training in the Lebanon at the hands of Iranian-backed Hezbollah. A Mahdi commander admitted sending 300 fighters known as the 'Ali al-Hadi Brigade' to Lebanon. The Iranian Revolutionary Guard also provided training for Iraqi Shia fighters in Iran, as well as providing logistical support. British intelligence assessed that the Iraqi Badr Organization retained 'strong links' with the Iranian Islamic Revolutionary Guard Corps, which funded, trained and armed the militia group, totalling up to 20,000 men. It was also suspected that Libya provided funding for Hamas and other Islamist attacks on Coalition forces in Iraq.

Then, in October 2006, the Mahdi Army fell out with its rivals – the Badr militia. In response to the death of Qassim al-Tamimi, provincial police investigator and also a key Badr figure, the blame was laid on the Mahdi. The latter attacked police stations in Amarah and took control of the city. This action almost pushed the whole country into all-out civil war.

By this stage US intelligence was assessing that the Mahdi Army was replacing al-Qaeda in-Iraq as the country's greatest cause of sectarian bloodshed. It was noted for having the most negative impact on the security situation, particularly in Baghdad and the southern provinces. According to an Iraq Survey Group report its membership had expanded from a few thousand after the invasion to around 60,000 by the end of 2006. The situation boiled over in the south in May 2007 when a local Mahdi leader was killed in Basra.

In fact, by early 2007 senior US officials considered al-Qaeda in-Iraq as the driving force behind the insurgency, not the Mahdi Army or the Badr militia. Its membership was estimated to number up to 10,000 men, making it the largest Sunni extremist group in Iraq. Nonetheless, the Iraqi military conducted Operation Charge of the Knights, striking at the Mahdi stronghold in Barsa in late March 2008. In response Mahdi-inspired violence spread across the country, including Baghdad, threatening al-Sadr's ceasefire. At the same time Iraqi and America forces moved against southern Sadr City to put an end to the mortar and rocket attacks being launched into the security enclave of the Green Zone. Finally, Muqtada al-Sadr agreed to a ceasefire on 10 May 2008 and permitted Iraqi security forces into the whole of Sadr City.

Although it appeared as if Iran's backing of the Shia/Sunni insurgency had failed, tragically, with the final withdrawal of US combat units in the summer of 2010, terrorist attacks continued in both Shia and Sunni neighbourhoods unabated.

Soldiers of the US 82nd Airborne patrolling the city of Fallujah in early February 2004 prior to a meeting with the city council. Known as the city of mosques, the blue domes in the background belied the violence about to engulf Fallujah.

Captured Iraqi insurgents. The old shell would have been used to make an IED if they had not been caught.

A Shadow 200 UAV used by US Army military intelligence to monitor Saddam loyalists, insurgents and foreign jihadists who pepped up their attacks on Coalition forces in 2004.

Hummers armed with TOW missiles and light armoured vehicles of the US 1st Marine Regiment photographed on 5 April 2004 cutting Highway 1 into the city of Fallujah.

US Marines laying down a deluge of fire. These men are from the 5th Marine Regiment engaging insurgents in Fallujah on 7 April 2004.

Armoured assault vehicle belonging to the 7th Marine Regiment, 1st Marine Division moves into Fallujah on 14 April 2004.

This USMC M1A1 was photographed during a mortar attack outside Fallujah in the summer of 2004, just before Operation Phantom Fury.

Members of the US 25th Infantry Division taking part in Operation Baton Rouge in Samarra in early October 2004.

Britain's Black Watch Battle Group supported US operations against Fallujah. These Warriors are involved in Operation Bracken Unit south of Baghdad.

The Black Watch at FOB Springfield on 7 November 2004.

Iraqi National Guardsmen in an unarmoured pickup operating with the US Marines to cut insurgents' lines of communication.

Operation Phantom Fury commenced against the insurgents holding Fallujah in early November 2004. This M109A6 Paladin from the US 1st Cavalry Division is lobbing 155mm shells onto enemy positions prior to the Marines moving in for a second time.

The AH-64 operating from forward operating bases (FOBs) offered a deadly combination of missiles, rockets and a chain gun in support of the Marines.

Marine 155mm towed howitzers were also involved in the initial barrage against Fallujah during the second offensive to clear the city.

A massive bomb flattens buildings held by insurgents on the outskirts of Fallujah. Air strikes also supported the attack by the US 1st Marine Division.

A Marine M198 medium howitzer laying down fire at Fallujah. The plan was simple: beat the insurgents into submission.

Fallujah suffered terribly at the hands of Marine firepower. None of the insurgent strongpoints could withstand a direct hit by an Abrams tank.

An M113 ambulance from the US 1st Cavalry rushes wounded from Fallujah on 12 November 2004.

US Marines and Iraqi Special Forces move through the devastated streets of Fallujah on 15 November.

A US Marine M1A1 blasts an insurgent strongpoint at point-blank range in Fallujah during the follow-up Operation New Dawn on 10 December 2004. Incongruously, the crew have left a blue plastic cool box on the top of the turret.

Snipers from the US 25th Infantry Division protecting an Iraqi police station in the northern city of Mosul on 17 November 2004, after an attack by insurgents.

Counter-insurgency operations were also conducted in mid-December 2004 in Mosul. This US 25th Infantry mortar crew at a FOB are providing supporting fire with a 120mm mortar.

A soldier from the US 25th Infantry keeps a close lookout for insurgents in Mosul in February 2005.

A US National Guardsman treats an Iraqi boy's high five with caution in Iskandriyah in early March 2005.

These AH-64 attack helicopters from the 101 Aviation Regiment are flying from FOB Speicher on 21 October 2005.

Even after the relatively successful pacification of Iraq's cities, attacks continued, driving an ever-widening wedge between the US military and the Iraqi people it was supposed to be protecting.

Chapter Ten

Phoenix from the Ashes

After the fall of Saddam Hussein the Coalition faced a dilemma. Foremost they wanted to ensure that the Iraqi Army would never again threaten the Iraqi people or Iraq's neighbours. The Iraqi armed forces, seen as servants of Saddam, were demobilized and sent home. Not only did this cause mass unemployment and fuel the insurgency, it meant that the security burden fell on the Coalition forces. When the Coalition began to form a new Iraqi Army no one wanted to see Iraq with powerful armoured forces again, but at the same time they could be a potent internal security tool. In terms of urban warfare there is nothing more intimidating than a tank parked on a street corner.

The rehabilitation of the Iraqi Army was a slow and painful process, tainted as it was by its association with Saddam Hussein's appalling catalogue of human rights abuses. Nonetheless, like the phoenix rising from the ashes, a new Iraqi Army eventually emerged to help fight the insurgency. Most notably, in mid-May 2006 the Iraqi 2nd Brigade, 9th Mechanized Division, assumed responsibility for security in the Taji area, and the Iraqi 2nd Brigade, 5th Division, began independent operations in Diyala Province. The Iraqi 7th Division was prepared to take responsibility for Al Anbar Province. The 9th Mechanized was the only Iraqi armoured unit with T-72 tanks and BMP armoured personnel carriers and was soon dubbed the 'jewel of Iraq' by military leaders.

During the handover ceremony for the 9th Mechanized, US Army Lieutenant Colonel David Thompkins, commander of 7th Squadron, 10th Cavalry Regiment (7-10), turned over responsibility to Iraqi Colonel Jamal Mal-Allah Ahmed. 'This is a great day for the 9th Mechanized Division,' said Iraqi Major General Ayoub Bashar, divisional commander. He added: 'A lot has been achieved by this young division, achievements that have done a lot to increase the division's combat capabilities.'

According to Lieutenant Colonel Thompson, men of the 7-10 Cavalry during the previous four months served as mentors and combat partners to the Iraqi 2nd Brigade. 'We have fought together shoulder to shoulder for the past few months against the enemies of a free Iraq,' he said. The 'Scorpions', a US military training team under US Army Lieutenant Colonel Carl Grunow, had also worked with the brigade since its formation in October 2005. At that stage the brigade had no armoured vehicles, personnel, weapons, uniforms or accommodation.

Most of the Saddam-era armoured fighting vehicles were destroyed in 1991 or 2003. What remained was largely unserviceable, having been starved of spare parts for more than a decade. To speed up the recovery the Iraqis were supplied Soviet-designed equipment, as this was what they were used to operating. Also, politically, the Washington-led Coalition felt it would be prudent to supply Soviet tanks rather than flood Iraq with American armour, which would only serve to irritate Iran and Syria.

In Iraq at Camp Taji, as well as a vast vehicle graveyard, millions of dollars' worth of armoured vehicle spare parts from the Saddam regime were discovered abandoned in warehouses. The American and Iraqi military set to work to categorize the parts for re-use with the Iraqi Army's 9th Mechanized Division. Enough refurnished vehicles were gathered to equip the division's 1st Brigade with a battalion of early 1960s-built T-55 tanks, plus two mechanized battalions of Soviet MT-LB armoured personnel carriers and BMP-tracked infantry fighting vehicles.

The Hungarian government came to the rescue at the end of 2004, donating seventy-seven T-72 tanks and 4 million rounds of ammunition. Another unspecified country offered 500 BMPs, although the Iraqis only accepted 100. Hungarian Prime Minister Ferenc Gyurcsány visited Iraq on 11 December 2004. In Al Hillah he saw the Hungarian transportation battalion that had served the Coalition for one and a half years. In Baghdad he then met with General George Casey, the commanding general of the Multi-National Force Iraq, and with Lieutenant General David Petraeus, the US Multi-National Security Transition Commander for Iraq, to discuss the fledgling Iraqi Army's needs. At his meeting with General Petraeus, the dual-hatted commander of the NATO Training Implementation Mission in Iraq, Gyurcsány reiterated the Hungarian decision to deploy troops, trainers and officers to the NATO mission in Iraq.

Refurbishing and shipping the Hungarian tanks cost Iraq's Ministry of Defence the bargain price of around $4.5 million. Once delivered, the T-72s and BMPs were used to equip the 9th Division's 2nd Brigade with two tank battalions and one mechanized battalion. After six months training in late February 2006, Iraqi T-72s of the 9th Mechanized Division began conducting operations in the streets of the Kadhamiya area of Baghdad. The following month, the 9th Mechanized, supporting the US 66th Armored Regiment, from the US 4th Infantry Division, conducted counter-insurgency operations near Halasba shortly after an improvised explosive device attack on a convoy.

In March 2006, the 2nd Brigade of the Iraqi Army's 7th Division received its first Humvees to replace the small, unarmoured pickup trucks it had been using. Members of the brigade graduated from a three-week Humvee licensing and preventive maintenance course at Camp Al Asad, taught by the US Marines. This qualified them to train and license fellow Iraqi soldiers within their command. The graduation ceremony also marked another milestone in the 7th Division's progress towards relieving Coalition forces in western Al Anbar Province.

During the handover for the Iraqi 9th Mechanized Division in May 2006 the US military training team and the 7-10 Cavalry made it clear that they would not simply turn responsibility over to the Iraqis and leave them on their own. Lieutenant Colonel Grunow said his team and its successor would continue to mentor and coach the Iraqi unit in training and in combat. The soldiers of the 7-10 Cavalry also continued to operate with their Iraqi counterparts in the region in order to bolster the Iraqi Army.

After the ceremony, Iraqi General Bashar said he was pleased with the unit's capabilities and proud of its soldiers. He said more and more Iraqi units were working to assume security responsibilities. By the end of 2006, all Iraqi divisions would be up and running and 'in the lead', he promised. Bashar told the soldiers of the 9th Mechanized that he had full trust in them to succeed in their mission.

On 12 May 2006, Iraqi soldiers of the 3rd Battalion, 2nd Brigade, 5th Division started independently conducting operations in their area of Diyala Province. They began gathering their own intelligence, patrolling the streets and hunting for insurgents and terrorists. A brigade-sized operation conducted throughout the village of Tahrir yielded a handful of suspected insurgents who were detained for questioning. 'They have been conducting operations on their own in this area under their young, charismatic brigade commander, General Saman al-Talabani,' said US Army Major Jeff Arrington of Multinational Corps Military Training and Transition Team. 'Talabani refers to himself as a modern general. Under the old regime, a general would not ask someone for their advice on how to do something. Talabani inquires how to do things better.'

The new Iraqi Air Force faced a similar challenge. 'We are starting over,' said IrAF Chief of Staff, Major General Kamal Barzanjy, in early 2006. 'America has given us a lot of help, and we have already accomplished many things, but we need to keep growing.' Saddam Hussein's air force was allegedly the sixth largest in the world at the outbreak of the 1991 Gulf War, with almost 800 fighter aircraft, but by 2003, only about 100 of these were still deemed operational. When Operation Iraqi Freedom came to an end only about 50 per cent remained and most of these had been badly damaged by crude Iraqi concealment efforts. The IrAF's commander, Lieutenant General Hamid Raja Shalah al-Tikriti, was captured on 14 June 2003. The old Iraqi Air Force ceased to exist and its personnel, along with the rest of the Iraqi armed forces, were sent home.

A significant milestone was reached on 7 March 2006, with the opening of the first Iraqi air base at New Al Muthana, while the first all-Iraqi aircrew flew their inaugural mission on 28 November 2005. Members of the IrAF's No. 23 Squadron navigated their C-130E transport aircraft from Ali Air Base, near Nasiriyah, in southeast Iraq, to New Al Muthana Air Base (the refurbished West Baghdad International Airport air base). They also flew their first cross-border humanitarian mission in February, air-lifting five children to Turkey for eye surgery.

On display at the official opening ceremony at New Al Muthana were the fledgling air force's American-supplied C-130E transport aircraft and Russian-built Mi-17 transport helicopters. 'It is important for Iraqis,' said Major-General Kamal. 'It is important for them to see tangible results and co-operation. Building up an air force takes so much work, finance and dedication.'

'Now our Air Force supports the government and the people,' said Colonel Jabber. 'In the past the Air Force only supported Saddam. We are humanitarian now.'

No. 23 Squadron had first moved to New Al Muthana in January 2006. The base provided the foundation on which Iraq's air force could rebuild with help from its Coalition allies.

The Coalition Provisional Authority (CPA) announced in April 2004 that it intended to help build a new IrAF, which would have a border patrol and surveillance role. Efforts to rehabilitate the discredited old IrAF and create a new force commenced in mid-2004, when more than 100 former IrAF personnel were sent for training with the Royal Jordanian Air Force (RJAF) in Amman. By the end of 2004, the new IrAF was 500-strong, equipped with a variety of light aircraft divided between bases at Tadji and Baghdad.

It was decided by the CPA that a major general would command a revitalized Iraq Air Force based at the Air Headquarters in Baghdad, and would act as the Chief of the Defence Staff's senior air adviser. Also, the IrAF's air missions would be fully integrated into Coalition air activity through the Multi-National Force Iraq. The new IrAF was principally tasked with transporting the army, border policing and surveillance of national assets. It is also involved in intelligence, surveillance and reconnaissance operations.

The new IrAF first became operational in mid-2004 with a squadron of six ex-RJAF UH-1H Iroquois utility helicopters stationed at Tadji. They were tasked with border and coastal patrol, troop transport and search and rescue. The new IrAF acquired an initial tactical airlift capability in October 2004 using two ex-RJAF C-130Bs based at the Baghdad Air Station.

The United Arab Emirates provided the IrAF with seven Comp Air 7SL aircraft and four Bell Jet Ranger helicopters, which were flown by No. 3 Squadron. The latter became operational in April 2005 and is based at New Al Muthana. The first four 7SL arrived at Basra Air Base on 13 November 2004.

Similarly, Jordan has also supplied two Seeker SB7L-360 and sixteen CH2000 light reconnaissance aircraft that are equipping No. 70 and No. 2 Squadrons.

A follow-on order was anticipated, but instead the new IrAF opted for sixteen US SAMA CH2000. Jordan Aerospace Industries manufactured these aircraft under licence from the Canadian Zenair Company (which builds the Zenair Zenith 2000) and delivered during 2005. The CH2000 Military Tactical Surveillance Aircraft (MTSA) variant is a two-seater trainer equipped with infrared thermal imaging and daytime TV camera. Half the CH-2000 equip No. 2 Squadron at Kirkuk Air base.

In the face of the escalating security situation, from November 2005 the United States Air Force (USAF) in theatre worked to stand up the new IrAF as quickly as possible. The new IrAF suffered its first aircraft loss on 30 May 2005, when one of the 7SL crashed near Jalula, 80km north-east of Baquba, while operating out of Kirkuk Air Base. Unfortunately, fatalities included an Iraqi airman and four US servicemen. They were buried in Arlington National Cemetery. Iraqi Air Force Captain Ali Hussam Abass Alrubaeye, thirty-four, became the first Iraqi ever buried at the United States' national military cemetery.

It seemed, post-Saddam, Iraq would abandon its Soviet aircraft legacy. However, the new IrAF is flying Soviet-designed aircraft. During 14-17 February 2006, eight former Polish Mi-17 Hip helicopters were delivered to New Al Muthana by a Russian An-124 transport aircraft. Reportedly, these were the first systems that the IrAF had acquired directly without CPA funding. The IrAF intended to be operating a total of twenty-four Mi-17s by mid-2007 from Taji Air Base in a deal worth US $105 million.

A symbol of new-found military muscle, a Iraqi T-72 tank guarding a street junction in the Kadhamiya area of Baghdad in late February 2006.

This Iraqi tanker is manning the turret-mounted machine gun ready for potential car bombers. Iraq's new armoured units were soon deployed in support of the counter-insurgency operation.

To speed up the recovery of Iraq's armed forces they were re-equipped with Soviet-designed weaponry. Hungary donated seventy-seven T-72 tanks such as this one, at a cost of $4.5m.

Second-hand BTR and BMP APCs were also donated to the Iraqi Army. This armoured column is operating with the US 4th Infantry Division in early 2006.

Freshly delivered Humvees waiting to be issued to Iraqi Army units. These were used to equip Iraq's 7th Division in March 2006.

On parade – a chilling echo of the days of Saddam Hussein's rule. Iraq's new T-72s were used to equip the 9th Mechanized Division, which first went into combat in early 2006.

Refurbished Iraqi T-55 and MT-LB. It's enough to remind you of the old days.

A refurbished Iraqi BMP-1 from the 9th Mechanized conducting street patrols with US forces.

A Hungarian-supplied T-72, now serving the 2nd Brigade, 9th Mechanized Division, along with an Iraqi M113, being put through their paces en route to Camp Taji in May 2006.

Iraqi Army Humvees making their presence felt on the streets. It took time for the new Iraqi units to slowly assume responsibility for security across Iraq.

Confident-looking Iraqi Military Police equipped with Polish-supplied DZIK-3 armoured utility vehicles.

Russian-supplied Kraz 7½-ton lorries waiting to be issued to their new owners.

Iraqi troops manning a joint checkpoint with US forces.

Grinning Iraqi tank crews undergoing training with the 9th Mechanized Division.

A symbol of Iraq's recovering military confidence – though behind the scenes it was acknowledged that tanks had little long-term utility against insurgents. Their real role was to act as a deterrent to Iranian aggression.

Chapter Eleven

Where did it all go Wrong?

American combat operations officially came to an end in the summer of 2010 with the withdrawal of the US 4th Stryker Brigade, 2nd Infantry Division. This formally heralded the end of Operation Iraqi Freedom and the commencement of Operation New Dawn, under which residual US forces assumed a training role. While the Iraqi armed forces were supposed to shoulder the full burden of maintaining law and order, vital American support still lurked in the background.

The US withdrawal from Iraq was one of the largest logistical operations since the Second World War. At its height America had 170,000 troops deployed at 500 bases across the country. The heart of the US presence was the Victory Base in Baghdad, once home to 40,000 troops and 20,000 contractors. Essentially it was a city within a city.

By late November 2011, there were only 18,000 US troops in-country and seven military bases still under their control. This dropped to 10,000 troops by mid-December. To complete the withdrawal Washington had to remove almost 3 million pieces of military equipment, valued at about $7.8 billion. At the same time, the US authorities scrapped tons of equipment as well as gifting redundant kit to the value of $390 million to the Iraqis.

In the run-up to the end of 2011, the highway south from Baghdad to Kuwait was nose to tail with American military convoys streaming south. Similarly, the skies over the Iraqi capital echoed to the constant drone of US aircraft shuttling in and out as gear was ferried home or to regional US bases. About a quarter of the materiel, which included vehicles, radios and weapons, was sent to Afghanistan to support security operations there.

When US Vice President Joe Biden visited Baghdad at the beginning of December 2011 to mark the US withdrawal, he was greeted by Sunni and Shia terror attacks. Just 50km north of the Iraq capital a car bomb killed ten people in the Shia town of Khalis. At the same time, gunmen attacked three houses belonging to former members of the Sahwa militia, Sunni fighters who had helped American and Iraqi troops take on al-Qaeda in-Iraq. Eight people were executed.

How Baghdad copes on its own long term remains to be seen. One thing is for certain: after eight years of war and more than 4,400 American dead and 32,000 wounded, Washington's enthusiasm for propping up the Iraqi government had ended. The UK called it a day after six years in 2009, when British troops finally withdrew from the southern city of Basra. This was at the cost of 179 dead and amidst much political acrimony over the legality of the war.

The real concern is that Iraq will come apart at the seams if its longstanding ethnic and sectarian tensions boil over. It is possible that anarchy is just around the corner. The Americans were able to act as moderators between the feuding groups, but with them gone, who knows what agreements will be honoured? Iraq's future remains far from certain or, indeed, stable. While the US has done all it can to strengthen the Iraqi military and police, it is unclear whether they will be able to keep at bay the Iranian-backed Shia militias and the al-Qaeda-linked Sunni militants. Indeed, many fear that America's withdrawal from Iraq will be seen as a long-term victory for Iran.

Certainly, US Senator John McCain believed that Iraq has been sacrificed to the public expediency of bringing America's troops home when the job had not been finished. McCain warned the US Senate Armed Services Committee that the completion of America's pull-out from Iraq would have 'serious negative consequences on the stability of Iraq and the national security interests of the United States'. He had a point and certainly no one wanted to see Iraq's vast oil reserves go up in flames.

After the American military pulled out, the Kurdish question loomed large, not only in Baghdad's mind, but also in Ankara, Damascus and Tehran. The economic and political success of Iraq's autonomous Kurdistan Regional Government (KRG) emboldened the Turkish Kurdish Workers party, better known as the PKK, to renew its attacks on Turkey's security forces. The KRG has shown what Kurdish aspirations can achieve and it is no secret that the Kurds are one of the world's largest ethnic groups without statehood. Like the Palestinians, the Kurds, whatever they say publicly, are working towards full independence. Turkey, Iran and Syria understandably oppose this with vengeance as they all have sizeable Kurdish populations.

Initially it was assessed that the oil-rich Iraqi city of Kirkuk would be one of the main flashpoints once the US security umbrella had been removed. Although this city is outside the Kurdish autonomous zone, it has a sizeable Arab and Kurd population – relations between the two there have been fraught in the past.

Although Iraq's armed forces have greatly improved with US training and equipment, the Iraqi government feared that the loss of US air support and intelligence assets permitted a resurgence of militants in the north and west of the country. In the weeks preceding the US pull-out, Sunni militants began testing the Iraqi security forces by targeting the Shia religious festival of Ashura. As a result, Shia were killed and wounded in al-Nila, Hilla, Khalis and Latifiya. At the same time, members of the Sunni militia who support the government were attacked.

Iraq's armed forces ordered $8 billion worth of American weapons, including artillery, tanks and jet fighters. Whether it will do them any good remains to be seen. They will need help to assimilate this hardware as well as a steady flow of oil revenue to pay for it.

Iraq was blighted by the eight-year-long Iran-Iraq War, two briefer Gulf wars and the subsequent insurgency. The question remains, can it now find peace and prosperity? It has the oil wealth to do so; it's just a matter of political will. Ultimately, only the Iraqis and the Iranians can answer that question.

British Paras in their moment of triumph in Basra on 7 April 2003. Operation Telic, Britain's contribution to Operation Iraqi Freedom, was a textbook mission. Objectives were secured swiftly and efficiently, with minimum casualties.

A British commando on guard in Baghdad in the summer of 2004. The swiftness of the Coalition victory caught everyone by surprise. What followed was a diplomatic and security disaster.

A potent symbol of US military power on the streets of Iraq. Despite this, the insurgents drained America's commitment to a new Iraq and by the end of 2011, the US military had withdrawn, having lost 4,400 dead.

A British tank supporting 40 Commando in the summer of 2004, trying to seek shelter from the midday sun. Britain's involvement in southern Iraq became a running sore.

A Black Watch Warrior crew proudly displaying their Scottish heritage in October 2004 during Operation Bracken. Britain lost 179 dead in Iraq.

US Strykers in the city of Mosul in October 2004 searching for Saddam loyalists during Operation Block Party. The metal grills are designed to ward off RPGs, which illustrates the constant level of threat from such weapons.

'Hearts and minds'. A Royal Marine from 40 Commando photographed in the summer of 2004 giving water to a young Iraqi boy. Five years later, Britain withdrew from Iraq to concentrate on operations in Afghanistan.

With the development of the Predator and Reaper, for the first time Iraq saw the extensive use of unmanned aerial vehicles, or drones, in the war against the insurgents.

A Predator UAV being prepped to hunt Iraqi insurgents. This was used to gather intelligence and as a platform from which to launch missile strikes.

The new face of modern warfare. The RQ-1 UAV and its successors have come to epitomise the so-called war on terror.

Chapter Twelve

What Happened to Saddam's WMD?

I n the wake of Operation Iraqi Freedom scant evidence of Saddam's WMD emerged. In late April 2003, US forces discovered a single suspected mobile biological weapons facility. Everything else proved to be a false lead. Nevertheless, it seemed to have passed the world by that just prior to Operation Iraqi Freedom notable evidence of Iraqi activities had been unearthed.

Despite Iraq's claims that it had destroyed its biological weapon (BW) spray tanks and unmanned aerial vehicles capable of delivering anthrax, some of these were discovered undeclared and intact by inspectors from the United Nations Monitoring, Verification and Inspection Commission (UNMOVIC) just before the Coalition invasion. Additionally, Iraqi claims that they had blown up all their 'iron' bombs containing BW proved untrue as numbers were unearthed intact.

The CIA stated in October 2002:'Iraq already has produced modified drop tanks that can disperse biological or chemical agents effectively. Before the Gulf War, the Iraqis successfully experimented with aircraft-mounted spray tanks capable of releasing up to 2,000 litres of an anthrax simulant over a target area. Iraq also has modified commercial crop sprayers successfully and tested them with an anthrax simulant delivered by helicopters.'

For some unexplained reason, Hans Blix, head of UNMOVIC, failed to brief the UN Security Council on a series of significant discoveries. Hidden in an addendum to UNMOVIC's *Unresolved Disarmament Issues – Iraq's Proscribed Weapons*, dated 6 March 2003, it emerged that modified aircraft fuel tanks had been found at Khan Bani Sa'ad airfield in December 2002. They were apparently part of an indigenously manufactured agricultural spray system developed for the IrAF.

According to UN sources, Iraq developed the Zubaidy spray system to deliver chemical and biological weapons (CBW) for the IrAF or the Iraqi Army Aviation Corps. It was first tested at Khan Bani Sa'ad in August 1988 using a Mi-2 helicopter spraying *Bacillus subtilis* (an anthrax simulant). One former UNSCOM BW inspector recalled that Khan Bani Sa'ad was a desolate place in the mid-1990s and that the crop sprayers were not in evidence then.

In contrast, in late 2002 the UNMOVIC inspectors found thirty ancient Mi-2. At the time UNMOVIC made no mention of the discovery of modified aircraft fuel tanks. What is not clear is whether they were part of the helicopter-mounted Zubaidy system or were those developed for the IrAF's Mirage F-1s.

Further damning Iraq, the UN issued videotape of an IrAF F-1 jet fighter conducting test dissemination of BW (1,000 litres of *B. subtilis*) from a modified drop tank over Abu Obeydi Air Base in January 1991. F-1 trials were in fact held twice in December 1990 (using water/potassium permanganate) and twice in January 1991 (using water/glycerine and *B. subtilis*). The Iraqis by their own admission had intended to produce twelve spray tanks but only managed four, which they claim were destroyed in mid-1991. If the ones found at Khan Bani Sa'ad were from the same programme then clearly the Iraqis lied about the destruction.

Previously Iraq contended that it had only conducted static BW agent tests using iron bombs at Muhammadiyat chemical weapon storage facility. Admissions about Abu Obeydi Air Base and Khan Bani Sa'ad are much more incriminating about the scale of the BW programme.

The Iraqis also attempted to convert L-29 jet trainers into UAVs, again fitted with CBW spray tanks, with unmanned test flights conducted in 1997. UNSCOM monitored the L-29, located at Samarra East Air Base, until its expulsion the following year. The March 2003 UNMOVIC report, detailing the spray tanks, also revealed inspectors had found an undeclared 7.45-metre-long drone. According to Washington, Iraq failed to declare this, two UAVs and the modified L-29 jet trainer.

The CIA judged that 'Baghdad's UAVs – especially if used for delivery of chemical and biological warfare agents – could threaten Iraq's neighbours, US forces in the Persian Gulf, and the United States if brought close to, or into, the US Homeland.' The discredited British dossier published on 24 September 2002 assessed that Iraq had 'developed mobile laboratories for military use, corroborating earlier reports about the mobile production of biological warfare agents; pursued illegal programmes to procure controlled materials of potential use in the production of chemical and biological weapons programmes.'

Additionally it noted the British Joint Intelligence Committee (JIC) had 'confirmed its earlier judgements on Iraqi chemical and biological warfare capabilities and assessed that Iraq has the means to deliver chemical and biological weapons.' All this was in clear defiance of UN resolutions for Iraq to disarm its WMD.

Saddam's regime claimed it had destroyed all its DB and R-400 biological bombs at an unrecorded airfield in mid-1991. After the arrival of UNMOVIC, Baghdad 'remembered' that Al Aziziyah Airfield was the destruction site. A UNMOVIC inspection team were presented with a vast, partly water-filled crater, which they ordered excavated. In late February 2003, the Iraqis retrieved two R-400 biological bombs (one with liquid contents) plus the remnants of another 118. By early March they had dug up a total of eight complete bombs, comprising two liquid-filled R-400s and another six empty ones.

Closer investigation of the destruction site determined the total number of BW bombs destroyed and assisted efforts to determine how many DB/R-400s were actually produced. During the mid-1990s, UNSCOM destroyed 3,469 DB-0/2 and R-400 BW bombs and related components.

The Iraqis, trying to stave off war and increase the rifts in the UN at a meeting with UNMOVIC in Baghdad on 8-9 February 2003, surrendered papers regarding anthrax and growth material, the nerve agent VX and missile production. One document suggested that some 1,000 tonnes of chemical agent were 'unaccounted for'.

Whilst it was widely reported that Serbia helped upgrade Iraq's air defences, what was not generally known was that Iraq diverted some of the equipment. In 1998 UNSCOM was aware that Iraq was up to no good with SA-2 surface-to-air missiles and al-Samoud surface-to-surface missiles, but had no idea of the number of engines Baghdad had managed to get its hands on. According to UNMOVIC, Baghdad illegally received 380 SA-2 missile engines. They were destined for use in the al-Samoud 2 missile system, which was assessed to be a proscribed weapon. UNMOVIC's response was to order the missiles' destruction just before Operation Iraqi Freedom.

Clearly Iraq simply lied and constantly back-peddled to cover the extent of its CBW and ballistic missile programmes. Furthermore, Baghdad deliberately concealed equipment it claimed destroyed in order to safeguard it for future use. Limited progress was made by UNMOVIC, no thanks to the Iraqis. However, much of it remained as Saddam Hussein wanted – that is, unaccounted for.

Not all of Baghdad's R-400 bombs were destroyed; potentially only a third of them were accounted for at Aziziyah. UNSCOM experts assessed that Baghdad's declarations vastly understated the production of biological agents and estimated that Iraq actually produced two to four times the amount of agent it acknowledged producing. These agents remain unaccounted for.

It also emerged that Iraq deliberately overstated its expenditure of chemical bombs by up to 6,500, and not 5,000, as previously reported, in order to conceal stocks. Similarly, equipment illegally imported to assist Iraq's air defence forces was diverted to its ballistic missile programme. It remains evident that UN sanctions and inspections did not work; only the threat of war forced the painfully slow flow of far from complete Iraqi admissions.

These revelations indicated to Washington and London that their suspicions were well founded and, in the face of Iraq's persistent refusal to unilaterally disarm its WMD, took appropriate action on 20 March 2003. Once the dust settled after Operation Iraqi Freedom, the Iraqi Survey Group (ISG) set to work hunting down Saddam's WMD scientists and his remaining stocks. Controversially, whilst the Iraqi scientists came quietly and captured files proved intent to resurrect programmes when the time was right, of the missing stocks there is no sign, although there have been many red herrings. It seems perhaps that all along Baghdad could have been telling the truth when it claimed that Saddam's WMD had been destroyed in the aftermath of the first Gulf War in 1991.

It was clear trouble was afoot as soon as David Kay, head of the ISG, announced his intention to step down amidst mutterings to Congress that the intelligence community had got it wrong. After resigning his post in January 2004, Mr Kay stated he did not believe there had been large-scale production of chemical or biological weapons since 1991. Damagingly, he told the US Senate Armed Services Committee, 'We were all wrong and that is most disturbing,' and called for an inquiry into the intelligence used to justify the war. To compound matters, former US National Security Adviser Condoleezza Rice accepted that there were flaws in the pre-war intelligence. US Secretary of State Colin Powell subsequently claimed he did not know if he would have supported the war if he had known there were no stockpiles. George Tenet, the CIA's director at the time, reacted defensively by saying his agency never claimed Iraq was an 'imminent threat'.

All intelligence is based on best available evidence and between 1998 and 2003 it seemed Saddam Hussein was up to no good. It must be remembered that Iran's similar assessment of Saddam's intentions had driven its own nuclear programme, adding further to the instability in that part of the world. The fact that the 12,000-word WMD dossier submitted to the UN by the Iraqis in October 2002 contained nothing new did little to exonerate them, but simply added to the fog of uncertainty.

A year later, the ISG's first report detailed Iraqi attempts to disperse or destroy evidence and intimidate inspectors. The group discovered that the Iraqi Intelligence Service (IIS) had run a 'clandestine network of laboratories and facilities'. It concluded concealment continued even after Operation Iraqi Freedom ended. Nonetheless, no WMD were found and it failed to find any significant evidence that Iraq 'undertook significant post-1998 steps to actually build nuclear weapons or produce fissile material.' It also concluded that Iraq did not have a large-scale chemical weapons programme after 1991. It seems the intent remained, but not the physical stocks of WMD.

However, everyone had short memories. In the face of American U-2 intelligence surveillance flights in early 2003, the Iraqis began to regularly move sensitive materials into the poorer districts of Baghdad. It was Saddam Hussein who refused to allow his scientists to co-operate with the UN's renewed inspection regime. The UK even offered asylum to Iraqi scientists if they agreed to be debriefed in Cyprus. This refusal was understandably seen as further evidence that Iraq did have something to hide after five years of being left largely to its own devices.

A number of Iraqis involved with Iraq's chemical weapons programme were murdered in the run-up to war. For example, former Iraqi Air Force General Ali Hussein Habib, who agreed to be interviewed privately by UN inspectors, was arrested just before the bombing of Baghdad. His body was found decapitated. Similarly, Khalis Mushin al-Tikriti, who worked for the Special Security Organization's (SSO) scientific department, reportedly oversaw the concealment of chemical weapons just before the arrival of the UN inspectors in November 2003. He was subsequently executed. However, reports that Dr Rihab Taha (also known as 'Dr Germ'), a leading Iraqi BW scientist, was assassinated on 31 January 2003 proved unfounded. She ended up in American custody. All of this illustrates the intense pressure the Iraqi military scientists were under from the regime. Unfortunately, the key figure in Iraq's nuclear programme, Khalid Ibrahim Said, was killed in April 2003 after running an American roadblock.

On top of this, Iraq's al-Samoud ballistic missiles violated UN restrictions and it was only after considerable international pressure that Saddam agreed to destroy them. Iraq also recommenced digging up its old R-400 biological bombs but remained vague on exact numbers. The ISG subsequently discovered that the Iraqis were converting SA-2 surface-to-air missiles into ballistic missiles with a range of 240km and were developing missiles with 480-1,300km ranges, all in violation of the UN.

It was clear that at some stage Saddam intended to resume his nuclear weapons programme. The International Atomic Energy Agency, tasked with verifying the end of Iraq's nuclear weapons programme, were particularly concerned about the disappearance in 1998 of 32 tonnes of HMX high explosives, which could be used to trigger a nuclear device (the Iraqis claim it was mixed with sulphur to make industrial explosives). Mr Kay intriguingly said he believed the ISG found 85 per cent.

David Kay aptly summed up the difficulties when he pointed out that corruption and secrecy in Iraq meant it was almost impossible to get accurate and verifiable intelligence. Exiles clearly had an agenda – top of which was the removal of Saddam. At the same time, Saddam's regime bears much of the responsibility for its own downfall. The lack of true transparency over his WMD meant that Saddam played a dangerous game of bluff; all the time that there was some question over his WMD stocks, he remained the strong man of the Middle East facing off America. Just as importantly, this stance also served to keep Iraq's mortal enemy, Iran, in check. Additionally, fear and incompetence added to the impression that Baghdad was being deliberately obstructive.

Ultimately, the truth is that the WMD issue mattered little; to the US administration the war was about regime change and gaining a new foothold in the Middle East to compensate for hostility to America's presence in Saudi Arabia. Additionally, Iran, Libya, North Korea and Syria were all served notice that WMD proliferation would not be tolerated. The message was received loud and clear after Gaddafi's Libya denounced its past activities. The question of whether Saddam should have been left to his own devices if he had no WMD stocks has to be answered with a resounding no.

There was a fear that Saddam might deploy a residual WMD capability in 2003. Shown here are the results of an Iraqi Scud missile attack during Operation Iraqi Freedom; thankfully, it did not have a chemical weapon warhead.

The man who brought the world down round his ears. Saddam Hussein was finally captured on 13 December 2003 by Task Force 121 and elements of the US 4th Infantry Division.

A US soldier examining an Al-Samoud ballistic missile. The Iraqis were working on a longer-range missile than this, which could have carried a chemical weapon warhead.

A Royal Marine checks an Iraqi car. Initially it was feared that Iraqi weapons of mass destruction would be smuggled into Iran, Syria or Jordan by al-Qaeda.

Captured Iraqi mortar bombs. Ultimately, tracking down Saddam's WMD proved to be a wild goose chase.

In contrast, Iraq was awash with conventional weapons. An Iraqi soldier and a US marine survey artillery shells, mortar bombs, landmines and small arms ammunition seized in the Fallujah area in 2005. These helped fuel the insurgency and were a public menace.

The shattered remains of a car bomb. Iraqi insurgents had no problems laying their hands on explosives, some of which even dated from the Iran-Iraq War.

These US explosive
ordnance specialists are
about to destroy a
sizeable stack of Iraqi
shells and landmines.

US Military Police on the streets of
Baghdad.

Defiant to the last. Saddam on trial – the Iraqi Interim Government executed him three years after his capture.

Intelligence from 1998-2003 indicated that Iraq was up to no good with its WMD programme. Subsequently, the Iraqi Survey Group, which scoured Iraq, found no evidence of ongoing chemical or nuclear weapons programmes.

Epilogue

The tenth anniversary of the US-led invasion that successfully crushed the Iraqi military within a matter of weeks was marked on 20 March 2013. In reality, both British and American forces knew that the invasion was a result of unfinished business following the liberation of Kuwait in 1991. The British Army conducted a textbook operation in securing southern Iraq and its oilfields, with minimal losses, in 2003.

Ultimately, whether Britain was right in joining the US-led invasion is subjective. Even former Prime Minister Tony Blair has admitted that Iraq did not turn out as he hoped it would. Personally, I was and still am convinced it was the right thing to do. However you looked at it Saddam's Iraq was unable to live by accepted international norms.

Under Saddam the Iraqis stormed into Iran, sparking an eight-year bloodbath, then attacked the Kurds and invaded and occupied Kuwait as well as massacring the Shia Marsh Arabs. He used chemical weapons against the Iranians and the Kurds with impunity, in spite of the huffing and puffing of the international community. He also threatened Israel with the prospect of an Iraqi nuclear bomb and the spectre of ballistic missiles delivering Iraqi chemical weapons.

There can be no denying that Saddam, his sons and their Ba'athist cronies treated Iraq like their personal medieval fiefdom, where they could take what they wanted. The real question is why this monster was left in power for so long. The reality is that there have always been simply too many monsters for the international community to keep on removing.

Most dictators eventually come to a sticky end or flee into exile – just think of Uganda's Idi Amin, Romania's Nicolae Ceaușescu, Ethiopia's Mengistu Haile Mariam, Libya's Gaddafi … the list goes on. Ultimately Saddam was the architect of his own downfall thanks to his endless wars and constant brinkmanship. All his posturing and obstruction of the UN monitoring regimes convinced the international community that he still had sizeable stocks of WMD. Ironically, after decades of war, Saddam proved to be a paper tiger.

Morally the problem with the US-led invasion was that it was based on a lie. Downing Street provided poorly presented intelligence that lacked the normal checks and balances of the Joint Intelligence Committee and the Defence Intelligence Staff, both of which up until that point prided themselves on the impartiality of their assessments being free from political interferrence.

Former Prime Minister Tony Blair took the country to war with Iraq in the conviction that he was 'right', not on the basis of sound intelligence. When Blair spoke of his conviction, he meant it as an act of faith – not a conviction in the legal sense of an irrefutably proven case. Once he had committed himself to US President George Bush, that was it.

It is worth remembering that Blair took the UK to war no less than five times, culminating with Iraq. He was a resolute interventionist. The threat to British interests in Cyprus from Iraqi ballistic missiles was grossly over-egged to justify British involvement. Likewise, Saddam's links with al-Qaeda were simply unfounded.

The Hutton Inquiry subsequently cleared Blair's government of 'sexing up' the September Dossier (*Iraq's Weapons of Mass Destruction: The Assessment of the British Government*) published in September 2002. The inquiry took place in 2003 after the invasion of Iraq had taken place – a case of closing the stable door after the horse had bolted.

The September Dossier was based on reports from the JIC and the key issues centred on Iraq seeking uranium from Niger and Iraq's ability to deploy weapons of mass destruction within forty-five minutes. Allegations by the BBC that the government had deliberately sexed up the dossier led to the suicide of the much respected Dr David Kelly, a biological warfare expert and former UN weapons inspector.

Kelly was well known and highly regarded by the intelligence community and they should have come to his rescue. He was a man of integrity and yet the the MoD allowed him to became a convenient scapegoat. The furore over his death in part distracted the public from the veracity of the document. Afterwards the media were of the view that the Hutton Report was a complete whitewash.

While the invasion went like clockwork, heralded by the US military's 'shock and awe', picking up the pieces proved far more problematic. Like former Yugoslavia, Iraq in reality is not really a unitary state and it had taken a dictator to hold it together, with all that that entailed. For Tito, read Saddam.

Having deposed Saddam, the Americans subsequently threw the baby out with the bathwater. On the grounds that all the Iraqi armed forces and police were Ba'athist party members, they were sent home, with predictable results.

There was a willful historical negligence by refusing to acknowledge that the co-operation of former Nazi party officials had been vital in running a defeated Germany in the immediate wake of the Second World War. Like former Yugoslavia, devastated Iraq will take decades to recover from the fall of Saddam.

Having successfully secured Basra in 2003, British troops soon found themselves the target of Iraqi and foreign insurgents, and losses began to mount. Our departure from Basra in 2011 felt more shameful than our arrival.

Disastrously, the key winner of international intervention in Iraq was Iran. Thanks to the elections, Iran's co-religionists – Iraq's Shia, who make up the majority of the population – now dominate the Iraqi Sunnis. It remains hard to see how sectarian violence in Iraq will ever die down.

Nonetheless, the mantra of risk-averse non-interventionists fearing what may come in the future seems a poor excuse for allowing the status quo to continue in the face of despotism.

Surely in the case of Iraq it was better to have acted than not acted at all? Operation Iraqi Freedom should be something to be proud of. What came after is a different matter.

Suggested Further Reading

Beck, Sara & Downing, Malcolm, *The Battle for Iraq: BBC News Correspondents on the War against Saddam and a New World Agenda*, BBC Worldwide, London, 2003.

Butler, Richard, *Saddam Defiant: The Threat of Weapons of Mass Destruction and the Crisis of Global Security*, Weidenfeld & Nicolson, London, 2000.

Collins, Tim, *Rules of Engagement: A life in Conflict*, Headline, London, 2005.

Conklin, Ryan A., *An Angel from Hell: Real Life on the Front Lines*, Berkley Caliber, New York, 2010.

Keegan, John, *The Iraq War*, Hutchinson, London, 2004.

Moore, Robin, *Hunting Down Saddam: The Inside Story of the Search and Capture*, St Martin's Press, New York, 2004.

Omaar, Rageh, *Revolution Day: The Human Story of the Battle for Iraq*, Viking, London, 2004.

Poole, Oliver, *Black Knights on the Bloody Road to Baghdad*, HarperCollins, London, 2003.

Ramesh, Randeep (ed), *The War We Could Not Stop: The Real Story of the Battle for Iraq*, Faber & Faber, London, 2003.

Rogers, Paul, *Iraq and the War on Terror: Twelve Months of Insurgency 2004/2005*, I.B. Taurus, London, 2006.

Ryan, Mike, *Baghdad or Bust: The Inside Story of Gulf War 2*, Leo Cooper, Barnsley, 2003.

Sifry, Micah L. & Cerf, Christopher (ed), *The Iraq War: Reader History, Documents, Opinions*, Touchstone, New York, 2003.

Simpson, John, *The Wars Against Saddam: Taking the Hard Road to Baghdad*, Macmillan, London, 2003.

West, Bing & Smith, Maj Gen Ray L., *The March Up: Taking Baghdad with the 1st Marine Division*, Pimlico, London, 2004.